HAUNTED HARROGATE

Paul Forster

Fisher King Publishing

HAUNTED HARROGATE

Print ISBN 978-1-914560-62-0
Epub 978-1-914560-63-7

Published by
Fisher King Publishing
fisherkingpublishing.co.uk

Cover illustration by Gareth Humphreys

Contents

Haunted Harrogate

In 1858, Harrogate was described by Charles Dickens as, "The queerest place, with the strangest people in it, leading the oddest lives of dancing, newspaper reading, and tables d' hôte." He wasn't wrong either. Even today, Harrogate attracts a wide variety of people from all walks of life. People travel from far and wide to visit the many events the town has to offer; from the Great Yorkshire Show to fantastic performances at the Royal Hall. Tourists love an outing to the Turkish Baths. You can step back in time and experience the wonder of Victorian architecture whilst enjoying the luxurious treatments they have to offer. Wandering The Stray or through Valley Gardens is a real treat; so lush and green. You feel as though you are in the countryside and not in a town centre. Strolling through the beautiful streets a visitor could be forgiven for not imagining that this beautiful place is haunted.

At the heart of the town stands the cenotaph; a solemn memorial to those who lost their lives in the First World War. Across the road is Betty's tearoom, which has an almost fabled reputation for wonderful service, scrumptious food, a place well worth a visit. There are a plethora of tea shops, restaurants and eateries in town and one of my favourites is The Harrogate Tea Rooms. This is housed inside the haunted Westminster shopping arcade, where we also find the fantastically named 'Curious Cauldron', a quirky shop selling Ouija boards, pendulums and all manners of oddities. We will visit this location later in the book.

Harrogate has a wealth of character, provided by a mixture of Georgian, Edwardian and Victorian buildings and plenty of green space making it a great place to explore. It was buildings of the town that inspired me to begin my journey into the paranormal of the location. My wife and I love ghost walks, and every holiday, we seek one out. When we moved to Harrogate, we were surprised to find there was no such tour. So, my wife suggested I start one. "There must be ghosts in Harrogate, it's old enough right?" she asked.

"I don't know if being an old town, means you find more ghosts or not?" I replied unsure of this statement. After much research and interviewing of local people, I had gathered enough stories to start a ghost walk and subsequently produce this book.

Most of the ghosts and hauntings found in Harrogate are predominantly from the Edwardian or Victorian era; due to our connection to both the first and second world wars we have a large number of soldiers and nurses from this period. Further afield, outside of the town centre you will find much older supernatural sightings such as spectral armies, civil war soldiers and ghostly monks.

Harrogate's spirits represent its population throughout time. We have some rather posh Victorian gentlefolk who haunt our grand hotels and plenty of phantoms who represent the working classes; from maids in public toilets to cleaners in hotels and lots of naughty poltergeists. We even have a room filled with ladies still enjoying a Victorian tea party. Harrogate is well and truly haunted both inside its many hotels, houses and bars and a few wandering the gardens and streets.

As we look beyond the boundaries of Harrogate we come across much older tales from the likes of Knaresborough and Ripley. Here, we find tales of Civil War soldiers, wandering monks and phantom hanged men.

Most of the stories in this book are known only to those who told them to me. This means that many of these tales will have never been published before. You are in for a real treat.

Harrogate is a place that I love and from which have carved a little niche out for myself. I started Harrogate's first ghost walk and I love guiding tourists and locals around our haunted spa town. My main income is through performing where I work as a mind reader at weddings, corporate events and parties. My main passion is writing and performing Victorian seances, where I use real stories and artefacts from the time period. I bring the stories to life through magic, mentalism and acting. On top of this, I also write copy for a great guy called Zach Greaves who introduced me to Rick Armstrong from Fisher King Publishing. So here we are. My first book, a collection of ghost stories from my beloved hometown of Harrogate.

Throughout my life and career I have had many experiences with the paranormal. Perhaps in another book I can talk about what I experienced but let's just say that I heard the footsteps of a former King of England, saw a poltergeist slam a door shut in a house visited by Shakespeare and had stones thrown at me in a prison cell beneath the city of Nottingham.

Prior to moving to Harrogate, my wife Francesca and I lived in London. The time came when we wanted to buy a house. We're both from County Durham so started to look North for a place to call home. We settled on Harrogate. After visiting only twice, we found the perfect four-story Edwardian house full of character and we got it. The house, thankfully, is not haunted.

To understand the paranormal, it is important to differentiate between the numerous types of hauntings and spirits associated with them. We begin by delving into some of Harrogate's most frequently experienced otherworldly activity. As we explore these different types of hauntings you will encounter some of my own personal experiences and stories.

Different Types of Ghosts

To understand what a ghost or spirit might be, we need to grasp the first law of thermodynamics; that no energy is created or destroyed in the universe. It has been proven scientifically that we, as living beings, are made of energy. Therefore, based on the first law of thermodynamics, our energy cannot die. When we die, our atoms that compose us remain behind. The electrical energy that pulses through our brains is what is left. Is it not possible that this energy contains memories, actions or moments from our life which are what we see as a ghost or paranormal activity?

Like a battery, energy can run out, if spirits and ghosts are made of energy then surely, they require charging? I believe that a lot of the hauntings in Harrogate are located near a water source, in particular, the spring waters which flow beneath the bedrock of our town. Places like Hales Bar, The Crown Hotel, Valley Gardens and The Turkish Baths for example, are all near a spring well or the waters flow underneath the building.

Through my research, I have come across a selection of different types of hauntings in Harrogate from poltergeists to full-body apparitions. I don't believe we will ever truly know why these hauntings take place but there are some theories as to why a spirit may be tied to a particular location. They may have died as a result of a traumatic event such as a murder or harrowing accident. It is often said that spirits remain on earth due to unfinished business. If you read the stories from Cedar Court Hotel or The Alexandra, it seems as though the spirits here do not know they are dead and are simply carrying on as if alive. Other theories suggest that a spirit hangs around to be close to a loved one, or they cannot rest due to an injustice done to them. Whatever their reasons, there is a wide selection of paranormal entities which haunt Harrogate. Here they are for your delectation:

Type of haunting: Shadow people.
Location: Hales Bar, The Royal Oak Knaresborough.

Shadow people are shapeless dark masses and are difficult to define as ghosts. They are often reported as being seen from your peripheral vision and usually vanish when you try to look directly at them. These manifestations have no features and do not appear in human form. In fact, clairvoyants consider them to be non-human and are associated with feelings of dread. These dark masses can move between spaces and usually follow a direct path of movement. They are also seen to almost dance uncontrollably in the space they inhabit. One such shadow person has been spotted moving though Hales Bar and is said to evoke feelings of dread or calm, depending on the viewer.

Years ago, my mam (I said I was from Durham) had an experience with a shadow person. She had a sewing machine in the dining room, where she would make costumes for the many musical theatre shows I performed in. She faced the arched doorway which led into the living room. From her position, she could sew and watch the television at the same time.

One day, she had the tv on and her head was down, concentrating on a particularly tricky piece of sewing. She thought she saw something out of the corner of her eye, like the top half of a child leaning out from behind the archway door. She quickly looked up and the figure had gone. For a moment she thought that perhaps she had mistaken something on the television for the figure, so she shook her head and went back to her work.

A moment later she noticed it again, out of the corner of her vision, a figure slowly leaning out from the archway. She kept her head down but moved her eyes up towards it. She thought she saw a little boy, just a shape with no features, but a little boy nonetheless. She looked up quickly but the thing had disappeared. My mam laughed and put her head back down. No sooner had she done this when the little boy returned. Once again she looked up fast, in order to catch sight of him but he was quicker than her and he vanished. She found herself playing peekaboo with the ghost of the little boy. She played for a few minutes then said, "Look, this is fun, but I need to get back to work." Seconds later, she heard someone light footed running up the stairs. My mam had come to accept that this little boy was haunting the house.

Type of haunting: Interactive Personality
Location: Harrogate Theatre, The Alexandra,
The Harrogate Club.

This is the most common type of ghost found in Harrogate. They are often seen as full or part body apparitions. They have a number of different styles in which they haunt. For example, take Hoopers store. Here, the ghost of a past employee emits the odour of cigar smoke, but in other hauntings the smell emitted could be anything from perfume to peppermint; as in Harrogate Theatre. Sometimes you will hear the ghost speaking, as so often happens in The Old Swan Hotel, or it may even try to communicate to you in person.

My mam told me that she had an experience with an interactive personality that she's never forgotten.

She said, "I was carrying a mattress upstairs, on my own of course, your dad never bloody helped." My mam is not someone to mess with, she is known to some people as 'Scary Jean' but I know her to be kind, artistic and a very talented costume maker. She continued, "I left the mattress at the end of the hallway just outside of our bedroom. I went back downstairs for something and when I went back up, there was this woman standing there. She wore a brown dress, she saw me, looked right at me, smiled and then disappeared. You remember one night when we'd come back from a rehearsal and your dad was sat on the wall outside?" She asked.

"Yeah, I remember." I said "We'd been rehearsing for a musical, right? And we came home and you told us to stay in the car. You went off to speak to dad and then you went inside."

"Well," Said mam, picking up her story again "I went in the house, turned on the lights in each room and looked around, went all the way up to the attic but didn't find anything."

"What were you looking for?" I asked.

"Dick." she said. We both laughed immaturely, but we do like a dirty joke. Dick was the former occupant of the house who had died years earlier. When the laughter subsided, she continued "Your dad said he'd come home from the pub and gone into the house."

She went on to tell me how he turned on the hall light at the bottom of the stairs. Then he heard a noise coming from upstairs. He shouted up for us all but no one answered. She told me he could hear a banging noise coming from deep within the house somewhere. He slowly made his way upstairs and checked each bedroom. Then the sound came again. It was coming from the attic.

He opened the heavy wooden door. 'Hello?' He called up. The only reply was a thudding sound. He ascended the stairs one by one. Slowly he got to the top and peered round the corner.

There, sat in his old chair was Dick. He was banging his foot up and down on the floor, as if to get his attention. Dick had been dead for years.

"Your dad crapped himself and ran out of the house. He was so afraid to go back in so he sat on the wall outside for a few hours until we got home. He made me search the house from top to bottom. Well, I got to the foot of the steep stairs to the attic and slowly made me way up. There was nothing there. Just the chair. After that we got rid of all his stuff and nothing happened again."

Type of haunting: The Poltergeist
Location: Hales Bar, The Cedar Court Hotel,
The Crown Hotel.

Poltergeist derives its name from the German word 'rumbling ghost' or 'noisy spirit'. Probably one of the most common types of hauntings in Harrogate, the poltergeist can move or knock objects over, create noises and manipulate the physical environment. A great example of this is in Hales Bar, where one such spirit moved some beer clips before the eyes of a number of patrons. Activity surrounding this type of haunting usually starts off slowly and builds in intensity. You may have seen the film of the same name, yet the poltergeist is supposedly one of the rarest and most frightening forms of hauntings. Loud sounds, objects being moved or hurtled across the room, doors slamming, lights turning on and off and even items disappearing only to reappear years later have all been recorded. The latter of these happenings was reported in the news when two antique candlesticks vanished from Ripley Castle in Harrogate, only to turn up years later.

I had an experience with a poltergeist when I was younger. In the room that I shared with my brother Michael, we had a tall wardrobe at the foot of my bed. Above it, we kept an assortment of games and a distinct red box that was full of felt tip pens. Whenever we wanted to reach them, we had to climb on our desk chair as we were too small to grab them.

One night, I was awakened by a sound. My eyes shot open and I stared at the ceiling above me. I waited for the noise again. "Stop it!" Whispered my brother.

"Eh?" I muttered in confusion.

"Stop it or I'll punch ya." Michael whispered threateningly.

"Stop what?" I asked, almost afraid to know the answer.

"Throwing pens at me."

From his bed he launched a hand full of felt tip pens across the room at me. I picked them up and studied them. I knew that they had come from the little red box on top of the wardrobe. I definitely hadn't thrown them. I knew that for sure as I was asleep. So, who had thrown them? My brother had already started snoring. I looked up at the wardrobe and shuddered, brought on by a sudden cold draught. I placed the pens on the floor by my bed, buried my head beneath the covers and tucked my feet into the bottom of the duvet to stop anything from grabbing them.

I soon fell asleep. In the early hours of the morning, the sun had already risen. I was woken by something unfamiliar. I lay there half asleep and then felt something tap my leg. I lay still, not knowing what was going on. Again, something dropped onto my leg, something small and light but with enough weight that I could feel it. I couldn't place what it was. I lifted the duvet off my head and took a peek. I was shocked to find four felt tip pens on my bed. I quickly shot a look at my brother, believing him to be the culprit, but he was fast asleep. Confused, I turned my gaze back to the bed and at that moment, I caught sight of a felt tip pen flying towards me from the top of my wardrobe. I looked up just to see its arched trajectory; I knew my brother hadn't thrown the pens. I didn't have a clue as to what was responsible.

Type of haunting: Orbs of light
Location: Mansion House, Harrogate Theatre and The Alexandra.

Orbs are usually seen, and often photographed, as balls of hovering or flying light. They are thought to be the physical energy of a spirit. A literal ball of energy, which is where they get their name. People often mistake dust particles as orbs, so they are the most commonly experienced supernatural event, when often it is not paranormal at all. If you were to witness an actual orb, or spirit light, you would see a ball of light with a solid centre mass which emits its own small amount of light. Orbs are often seen in places such as graveyards or where deaths have occurred. One example would be the spirit orb of light seen in Harrogate Theatre which is thought to be that of Alice, the theatre's ghost.

Type of haunting: Residual Haunting
Location: Cedar Court Hotel, The Crown Hotel and Valley Gardens

Thought to be a highly negative energy associated with a tragic event such as a murder. However, it can also be a very positive energy; a happy day such as wedding or party. Whether it is a bad or good energy, the hauntings are not intelligent and are not aware of their surroundings. The spirits simply go about their own activities, with no interaction with the living. This is known as the 'Stone Tape Theory', which is the held belief that spirits are simply moments in time recorded and played over and over again. A fantastic example of this is at The Cedar Court Hotel, where a room full of Victorian ladies were seen having high tea in a function room. Residual energy can be a visual haunting or an auditory experience, where the participant can hear music, laughter, footsteps or even full conversations taking place.

Ghost Stories

What comes next are a collection of eerie tales. Most are the personal accounts from those who experienced these paranormal events first hand, many of which have never been seen in print before. A small proportion of stories are from the annals of history and are well known locally. The Harrogate Ghost Walk starts it journey outside of the Royal Pump Room Museum, so it seems rather fitting that this is our first story...

Royal Pump Room Museum

The Royal Pump Room Museum is home to the strongest known sulphur well in Europe. It is also the starting point of the Harrogate Ghost Walk. In its heyday, it was a tourist hot spot, with over 15,000 visitors from across the world visiting every summer from the 1800s until its closure in the late 1940s. The rising popularity of Harrogate as a tourist destination saw a number of buildings crop up in order to meet the demand of visitors. One such establishment was the Royal Pump Room. This striking octagonal building began welcoming visitors in 1842. For a small charge, it allowed the well-to-do of Harrogate to enjoy the spa waters, protected from the elements.

Guests would promenade through the building whilst (despite the eggy smell of the sulphur), enjoying a glass of the healing waters. Music was performed by a live band which provided the perfect cover for those wishing to chat privately and gossip.

The working class of Harrogate were provided for too. A free tap provided drinking water in the street, across the road from Hales Bar. The tap is still there to this day and is protected by Act of Parliament. (The Stray Act 1985 provides - section 11 (1) (c) - *'The Council shall maintain and protect...the supply of water without charge from the public drinking fountain situate outside the Royal Pump Room.'*

Harrogate gained its very own 'season', from May to September, where the rich, famous, and wealthy would escape their usual haunts and come to Harrogate to enjoy all it offered. The aristocratic 'season' followed the traditional holidays or recesses of Parliament. Having its very own season was a huge boost to the local economy and it lifted the status of this Yorkshire town.

During these summer months, guests would visit the Pump Room between 7 A.M and 9 A.M. As well as taking the water, they would promenade outside in large numbers, play cards, hunt or even watch the horse races at the Stray racecourse.

Those who were seriously ill would remain inside and bathe in the waters, receiving around three weeks of treatments. The spa waters were hailed as a cure for a variety of ailments, including scurvy, epilepsy, and skin complaints such as ulcers, sores and rashes. After World War II, Harrogate's popularity as a spa town declined. The building which once boasted visits from the likes of Lord Byron, Russian Royalty, and Sir Arthur Conan Doyle, closed its doors. It has been used as a museum since it reopened in 1953.

The spa waters were used for years as a potential cure, but the healing waters of Harrogate may have properties we are yet to understand? Perhaps they can prolong your life long after death, for our first ghost resides in the museum itself.

In the summer of 1998, an American lady named Jayne Parker was visiting her sister who had moved to Harrogate some years previous. Jayne had the afternoon to herself whilst her sister ran some errands. She had always been interested in history and considered herself to be a bit of a histrophile. So much was her love for history that she volunteered in her home-town, providing guided history walks to tourists.

When Jayne heard about the Pump Room Museum, she decided to visit. The sun was shining, dappled light seemed to find its way into the museum, casting shadows which danced across the floor. It was warm, a little too warm for comfort. Jayne pulled at the collar of her t-shirt to release some of the heat. It didn't work. It was stuffy inside and she was already looking forward to taking a walk beneath the shade of the trees in Valley Gardens after her visit.

She imagined what it must have been like to promenade outside these walls during the Victorian era. She briefly imagined herself in a large dress, fanning herself and gossiping wildly with her fellow companions.

She was brought out of her daydream when she noticed something unusual. A mannequin of a well-dressed gentleman; in what she assumed was a Victorian suit complete with a black bowler hat atop his head, stood in the middle of the room. An odd place for a display she thought. It certainly wasn't there a moment ago when she entered.

Suddenly it moved. Startled, her hand flew to her mouth to stifle a little shriek. She must have been mistaken. Perhaps the shadows were playing tricks on her eyes. She held her breath as a number of thoughts flooded her confused mind in a matter of seconds. It occurred to her that it could be a costumed actor who worked there, perhaps he was a real person. Either that or she was dreaming. She was sure she hadn't seen what she thought she had.

She never could have been so wrong. She watched in utter disbelief and horror as the man walked with purpose towards a solid wall and disappeared through it. The moment the man, who was as real as me or you, dissolved through the brickwork was the moment Jayne ran from the room.

Jayne never told anyone of her experience and kept it a secret for years. It wasn't until she visited Harrogate in 2022 where she heard a similar story told to her by yours truly on the Harrogate Ghost Walk, that she realised what she had seen was indeed as she had thought. A ghost.

This full body apparition of a Victorian gentleman has not been seen by many, yet he has been seen none the less. Little is known about who the man was but one can only assume he was a visitor of the spa whose life has been extended into the spirit world by the healing waters of Harrogate.

Members of staff have reported feelings of being watched, sudden drops in temperature as well as a shadowy figure often seen out of the corner of your eye.

Hales Bar

Standing a few yards adjacent to the Pump Room Museum is Hales Bar, the oldest licensed premises in Harrogate. In my opinion, this is the most frequently haunted building in Harrogate.

This former coaching inn dates back to 1827 and was known then as The Promenade Inn. It grew in size over the years and by the time William Hales became the landlord in 1882, it was the pub we see today. Not much has changed, the building both inside and out remains true to its Victorian roots.

The single-story watering hole is wedged into the corner of a row of old buildings. To the rear is a courtyard and former coach house and stables. Built to last in good old Yorkshire stone, it is the architype pub you'd expect to find in any Yorkshire town. The frontage gives little away as to what horrors await inside.

A row of eye height windows look into the oldest part of the pub, allowing the inquisitive passer-by a sneaky peek inside. This smaller space is a Georgian style Vaults room. Refurbished in 2013, they uncovered the original wooden beams and a stone fireplace. There is even a small bar with a service bell, which we will come back to later.

Further along the front of the building is a rather large, arched doorway leading into the main part of the venue.

Stepping inside the pub is like stepping back in time. Dark wood panelling hugs the walls and blood red, leather clad seating booths invite you into their curved embrace. The room is dim due to the fact there are no windows in this part of the building. Every shelf and piece of wall space is swathed in a plethora of Victorian paraphernalia. It boasts a menagerie of taxidermy mammals and a wide assortment of curious photographs and pictures. In the far reaches of the bar is a private booth where you will discover a fanciful compendium of local history books.

The bars crowning glory are the atmospheric and original gas lamps and cigar lighters which cast an eerie glow across the bar top. A welcome sight to behold on a cold dark night. Hales Bar is special and really is worth a visit.

The old coaching inn has had a wealth of customers through its doors across the centuries. It has always been a popular drinking establishment. The working classes would drink from the sulphur tap at the royal pump room and then drink from an altogether different tap at Hales bar. Due to its long history and its position above the eggy sulphur waters below its foundations, it is no surprise that the building is incredibly haunted.

If you were to visit today, you would be welcomed by the current landlady, Amanda Wilkinson. Amanda was the youngest licensee in Harrogate, receiving her license at court at the age of 18. She took ownership of the bar around 19 years ago (as of 2022). As a young woman, she lived in the flat next door to the pub with her baby and her seven-year-old son, Ben. Amanda enjoyed living in the flat but her son Ben had an altogether different experience.

One night Amanda heard Ben upset in his room. She went in to find out what the matter was. "There's someone outside my door." He said though stifled tears.

"There's no one here but you, me and the baby." Came Amanda's soothing voice as she hugged him tightly.

"There was whispering." Said Ben in hushed tones.

"Whispering? Where?"

"Outside my door. Someone was whispering."

As she tucked him back into bed, Amanda explained to her son that he had probably had a dream and was to go back to sleep. "But who was the man outside my door?" Yawned Ben. "I saw him. He was white, a white shadow. Whispering and walking past my…" Ben's voice trailed off as he fell back to sleep.

The next day Amanda was speaking to one of the locals about the incident and he nodded. "Not the first time that's happened" he said.

"What? Someone's heard it before?" Asked Amanda incredulously.

"Oh aye. There're loads of people who've lived there have heard whispering and seen strange shadows. It's haunted."

As Amanda listened to further tales of ghosts and disembodied voices which apparently haunted both her flat and the pub, she was reminded of her first encounter with a ghost. At the tender age of sixteen, Amanda worked in Oliver's fish shop in Knaresborough. Turning up for work for each shift, you descended the dark stairs into the cold basement, where you would change from your day clothes into your work uniform.

The small basement had a low ceiling and thick walls. It was all but empty, except for a chair and some stock for the shop. In the corner was a recess, an old storage cupboard whose door had been removed at some point in the past. There was one light bulb hanging in the centre which cast a dim glow around the oppressive confines of the room.

Amanda had changed into her uniform many times down there. Always quickly but not out of fear; just because she didn't want to be down there on her own for too long.

One evening, a few months into her time working at the fish shop, Amanda was alone in the basement and had just changed into her uniform. She was just finishing tying her shoelaces when she paused. Something in the room had changed. Ice cold fingers ran up her spine, and the hairs on her arms stood on end.

She felt like… no, she knew she was no longer alone. She held her breath, waiting for the hidden stranger to reveal themselves. Looking around the dark, dank space, she saw nothing. Not at first. Her eyes were drawn to the cupboard in the corner. There, sat on an unseen chair was an old man. He sat watching her. Amanda was struck by his white face; his leering gaze locked onto her face. His black clothes gave no indication as to what era he had come from previously. Amanda knew what she was looking at. A ghost.

She ran from the basement and flew up the stairs. She hurriedly told her colleagues about the horrifying man in the basement and one of the men ran down to find the intruder, only to return to say the room was empty.

After the experience of coming face to face with a ghost, Amanda changed into her uniform before she got to work. She never returned to the basement again. However, she believes this experience is why, as an adult, she is not scared of ghosts. They simply don't bother her. She believes in their existence and has had enough paranormal experiences to write her own book, but Amanda is a no-nonsense kind of person.

She's worked in the food and beverage industry all her life and although she is kind, generous and outgoing, she is not someone who is easily perturbed.

She is warm and is absolutely passionate about Hales bar, its history, and her customers.

It will come as no surprise that the local drinkers who frequent her bar never want to leave. In fact, many of them remain there. Indefinitely. Above the bar are a number of curious cupboards. Inside one of these cabinets are the remains of seven regulars. No, there is nothing gruesome about this, it is a rather unusual tribute to her most beloved friends and family members.

Amanda's most loyal patrons are so passionate about the Inn that when they die, they leave some of their ashes to the pub. Amanda selects the colour of her mini urn to reflect something about the person whose ashes are to be interned inside. Each urn is placed inside a bespoke made, glass fronted cabinet above the bar where they can gaze down on their favourite watering hole. It's an honour for regulars to find a final resting place above the bar. Amongst the macabre collection is a loyal and much-loved member of her staff who passed away too early in his life and Amanda's stepfather.

Of course, when you have the ashes of dead people in your establishment, you open yourself up to be haunted. Hales bar, as mentioned earlier, is the most frequently haunted building in town. By that, I mean that it has the most activity. If you were to pop in there for a drink at any time of the day or night, it is highly likely that something unexplainable would happen.

That is exactly what occurs on a regular basis. As previously mentioned, the bar has no windows of which can be opened. In fact, the main bar area doesn't have windows at all. The front and back door are always kept closed. So why is it that Amanda keeps finding crisp white feathers in different parts of the building?

White feathers have appeared in stories and books for centuries. In Native American culture, their meaning was linked to a higher wisdom, peace, the end of misfortune and a new beginning after death. The appearance of feathers has long been linked to the spirit world and are associated with the divine connection to the other side. It is therefore believed that, if you find a white feather in a place where it seems unusual to find one, you are being communicated with by the spirit world.

Although Amanda is a no-nonsense woman, she believes this is exactly what these feathers symbolise to her. She often finds them on a morning, opening the backdoor, she is no longer surprised to find a crisp white feather waiting for her on the welcome mat. She takes this as a sign that the spirits behind the bar are saying 'good morning' to her. She has lost count of the number of feathers she has found and often puts it down to a message of remembrance from the seven little urns above the bar.

The strange appearance of white plumage is nothing

compared to the poltergeist activity experienced by bar staff and customers alike. In fact, I was in Hales bar one afternoon talking to Amanda, arranging a time for our interview about her hauntings, when a glass appeared to jump off a shelf. I waited for the inevitable smashing of glass. Nothing. Looking down to the floor, I was surprised to see the glass had landed on its bottom and was completely unharmed. A member of staff simply picked it up and put it back in its place. I looked at Amanda and asked "Does that happen a lot?"

"What the glass thing? Yeah, all the time. They're always jumping off the shelves and landing on the floor. They never break though. Not even the thin glasses. They just land there; we pick them up and put them back. Happens a lot." She replied matter-of-factly. This apparent poltergeist activity is not uncommon in Hales Bar. Glasses being moved by an unseen hand have been witnessed by staff and customer for years.

Suzi, one of the bar staff often feels a dark and unwelcome presence in the bar, mostly at night when she is alone and locking up. One evening, she swore she saw a shadow move across the floor of the empty pub but she simply put it down to a trick of the light. Suzi, like Amanda, believes in ghosts but always tries to justify and explain what she has experienced. For example, Suzi has misplaced many things: keys, pens, note pads, and other small items. She places them down and when she returns to pick them up, they have gone. Sometimes the objects have just been moved to another place in the pub. This, she can't explain.

The most unusual occurrence she witnessed was a tall glass which moved along the top shelf behind the bar, where it fell onto the hard floor below, bounced twice and landed on its bottom. She expected it to smash but it didn't.

Suzi has also witnessed a shadow figure floating through the main area of the bar. 'I wasn't scared. I just watched it, wondering what, or who it was.'

Irina, another team member, has worked in Hales bar for over six years. She has never seen or heard anything unusual herself, but she has witnessed the reaction of a group of people who did.

One evening she was alone behind the bar. A group of six women were drinking and talking in the private booth which had been reserved for them. Irina suddenly noticed their chatter had come to an abrupt halt and then they all screamed loudly in unison. Panicked by their sudden outburst of horror, Irina dashed over to ask what the matter was.

"There, on the shelf, they were moving." Pointed one customer. The lady was gesturing towards a shelf behind the bar where a number of beer clips were sat. The beer clips are advertising placards which clip to the front of a beer pump handle. "Those things there, they were flipping over and around all their own!" Gasped another woman, clearly terrified.

Irina, unperturbed, inspected the beer clips one by one and found nothing unusual. She gave the ladies a look which said, "You're pulling my leg." One of the women understood the look and replied "Honestly, they were turning over and moving around as if someone were stood there flipping them over."

The most frequent activity is the ringing of a service bell. In the oldest part of the pub is a small bar, often unstaffed. On the wall is a small button, press it and a bell will ring in the main bar area to call the attention of a team member who will duly walk through a door to the small bar to serve you. This bell rings of its own accord. Daily. A member of the team will enter the small bar area, look around to find it empty and return promptly back to the main bar. No one is sure who is responsible for the naughty activity, some believe a child is responsible, others think it could be Mary.

Mary is a ghost who could be as old as the pub itself, for there have always been stories about her. Amanda remembers, as a young lady, working at the pub as a cover manager. She was told stories back then about the ghost of Mary. One time a very old man came into the pub, Ben.

Amanda later found out that Ben was in his late 90s. He was a local and knew a lot of stories about the bar. Ben sat down and ordered his usual, after some pleasantries and small talk, he asked Amanda "Have you met Mary yet?"

"No, I don't think so, will she be coming in tonight?" Asked Amanda, assuming he was referring to another patron. He laughed

"No love, she's the resident ghost. Been around for as long as I remember." This was the first story about Mary which Amanda's had heard and there have been many more since.

No one actually knows who Mary is, all assume she was a local customer to the bar. We know that she is seen often. Staff and drinkers alike have borne witness to a strange black shadow floating across the centre of the room. This same dense black figure has been spotted lurking down the corridor which leads to the toilets.

It's not just the staff who have witnessed ghoulish activity. A local paranormal team investigating the bar caught a black shape floating behind an internal door on camera. Some believe that this shadowy figure is William Hales but one thing is sure, if you see it, you won't forget it.

If you visit Hales Bar, and I recommend you do, you may meet Zoe. She's not a ghost but Amanda's loyal companion. A friendly strawberry blonde Corgipoo, with a white muzzle and playful temperament who is often found snoozing in the private booth. However, often, when Amanda can't sleep; she finds herself drawn to the bar where she sits in the dark with Zoe and reads or listens to music.

One night, Zoe was curled up next to Amanda in the private booth. They were both enjoying each other's company and the solitude of the densely quiet bar. Zoe suddenly sat up. She darted a look towards the bar. Amanda followed her gaze and her eyes landed on nothing. Just the bar, as it always is. Something had unsettled Zoe, who jumped from her warm resting place and onto the cold floor. Zoe sat there, staring at the bar, ears pricked far back. She emitted a long, deep warning growl. "Zoe." Amanda scolded. "Stop it." Zoe continued her long low growl. A warning thought Amanda, who had turned her attention back to the bar. The place was empty, locked up tight. There was no one else here. Yet her little dog growled menacingly at the empty bar.

As quickly as she had started, she stopped. Hopped back up onto the chair and settled down again to sleep. Amanda, being the kind of person she is, thought nothing more of it. What do you think?

The atmosphere generated by the original gas lamps and Victoriana is unlike anything you can experience anywhere else in town. On the whole, it exhibits many ghostly manifestations and unusual poltergeist activity.

So, if you ever hold hope of having a paranormal

experience, then you'd be hard pressed to find anywhere more giving than Hales Bar.

Valley Gardens

Right beside Hales Bar is the main entrance of the town's much-loved park. When taking in the attractive and tranquil surroundings of Valley Gardens, you would be hard-pressed to believe it was haunted. The grounds were cleverly designed for visitors to the spa town to 'take the cure'. After spending time enjoying the healing waters at the Royal Pump Room, one would promenade through the leafy parkland as part of a planned health regime. The walk takes you alongside a meandering stream which snakes through the many trees, ornamental plants and well-manicured lawns.

The winding watercourse joins a small duck pond and beyond it is a large boating lake, that is still used today by toy boating enthusiasts. There is a quaint teahouse selling local ice-cream, and a bandstand which hosts festivals and events all year round. The gardens are always full of people and have been enjoyed by the public for decades.

An assortment of tall trees encircle the gardens like soldiers standing guard. Beyond these trees are elevated terraces of stylishly lofty houses. Rising high above the Sun Pavilion, the former Grand Hotel dominates the skyline like a stern Victorian Headmaster. We will visit this building later, for inside are some of the most frightening stories Harrogate has to tell.

Back in the gardens and to the left of the Sun Pavilion are the public conveniences. Even the toilets are nice on the eye. Built in 1924, the one-story block has a mock Tudor look to it, red stone walls and roof tiles to match. The gentlemen to the right and women to the left, they're a mirror image of each other. They nestle beneath a canopy of high trees and are tucked behind shrubs and a large pink cherry blossom tree.

Don't let their looks deceive you. For the ladies toilets appears to be in permanent use by that of a maid from the 1920s era.

In the summer of 1994, Kathy was enjoying a walk in the gardens with her husband, Barry. Nature called, so they made their way to the toilets. Kathy walked in and was hit by the sudden drop in temperature from the warm air outside. She shuddered. The air smelled fresh and she was impressed by the cleanliness of her surroundings. A few moments later, she was at the sink. No one had come in so she knew she was alone, but she couldn't push away the feeling of being watched. She looked around. Nothing. No one.

As she was lathering her hands, she became aware of a presence which wasn't there before. She turned and was taken aback to see a girl standing there. The young lady was pretty, with diminutive features. Her hair was slicked back tight and flat against her head. She wore a small white cap that had elastic hidden within the hem. She was dressed in a black skirt and white apron. Kathy smiled and turned back to rinse her soapy hands, and, in that moment, she noted that the girl was dressed in old fashioned clothing. Assuming she was part of a fancy-dress convention visiting town, she turned back round to admire the girl's costume. Only Kathy was alone again. She thought nothing of it, assuming the young lady had left without her noticing.

After drying her hands, Kathy left and looked around. Barry was taking shelter from the now burning midday sun, beneath the shade of a large tree. He noticed his wife was looking around. "Lost something love?" He asked.

"Did you see a girl come out here?" Came her quizzical reply.

"A girl? No. Just you. Why?"

Kathy looked around. "There was a girl in there with me. I saw her. She must have come out here." She turned and went behind the building for a moment. She came back and found Barry looking bemused.

"There was a young girl. Dressed in a costume, like a maid or something. She was in there. She must've come out here." Said Kathy, confused. She went back into the toilet block and looked inside each cubicle. Each was empty. There was nowhere to hide.

"Kathy." Barry shouted; his voice sounded further

away than it was. She exited the building.

"She must've come out of here and you've not seen her." She stated.

"Honestly, no one came in or out of there but you." Barry said. Perplexed, Kathy and Barry left to complete their stroll. They discussed the incident long into that night and eventually conceded that it could have been a ghost. They searched for similar stories but found nothing.

More recently in 2016, Jane was using the facilities whilst her partner Richard waited outside. The day was overcast and Richard was being kept amused by a cheeky looking squirrel darting along the grass, its tail hypnotically lolloping up and down. He turned to see someone exiting the ladies. Expecting his wife, he was taken aback to see a young, pretty girl. Her hair plastered flat against her skull, with a small white cap sitting atop her head. She was dressed in a black skirt and white apron. She was solid, as real as Richard was. He did a double take and she was gone. She was there one second and had vanished the next.

Richard couldn't comprehend what he had just seen. Confused, he looked around the immediate area, searching for the mysterious girl. He popped his head through the open door to the ladies and was accosted by his wife Jane who was now on her way out. "What are you doing Dicky?" She asked.

"Is there someone in there?" Came his confused reply.

"No there isn't. Just me." He moved past his wife and went inside, taking a quick look around, he was satisfied that it was empty.

"What are you doing?" Jane demanded.

"A moment ago, a girl dressed in old clothing came out. She looked like a maid. You know, from the Victorian times. She walked out from in there and I blinked, and she was gone."

These are the only two accounts I have come across in regard to any ghosts in Valley Gardens. What is interesting in this case is that the two stories match. The individuals involved were not known to each other and I believe this is the first time the story has ever been documented. What is more interesting is that one account takes place inside and the other sighting is outside.

So, who is the mysterious maid in the ladies' toilets? If we take in the description of the young girl, one would assume she was a Victorian maid. However, the toilets were not added to the garden until much later in 1924. If we look at the clothing worn by maids in the 1920s, they match exactly the description of this particular manifestation. Who knows why the young lady is bound to this location, perhaps she visited here every day? She could even have used the building to change from her everyday clothes into her uniform before heading off to work in one of the nearby houses or hotels. What is known is that water is all around this location, provided by the many spring wells in the gardens. Perhaps this water source provides the energy needed for this certain haunting.

Windsor House - Formerly The Grand Hotel

The former Grand Hotel building dominates the landscape on Cornwall Road, which overlooks the Valley Gardens. The building, which was completed in 1904 for Sir Christopher Furness, sits on the edge of the exclusive residential area known as the Dutchy Estate. The building has seven storeys including the basement. When it was a hotel, it also had its very own garage which could hold approximately 100 vehicles and was complete with a filling station.

The ground floor consisted of an imposing reception hall, a main lounge area, a French restaurant with aperitif bar, a grand bar with access to the grounds and an American style bar. There was a smoking or Billiards room, with billiards being the most fashionable pastime for gentlemen.

The lower ground floor was home to the grand ballroom and further bar area. Deep beneath the building was the boiler room and services.

Much of the layout of the current building remains the same, the building is now known as Windsor House. It has since been converted into offices and rented out by a number of different businesses. I was visiting the office of Zach Greaves (the man who would eventually introduce me to my publisher for this book.) Zach is a lovely guy, who runs a very successful digital marketing business. After we had finished our meeting, conversation turned to my ghost walk.

This in turn lead to Zach proclaiming that the building was haunted. "I'll introduce you to the buildings facilitates manager, Richard. He can tell you a few ghost stories about this place."

And he did. Richard was very generous with his time and took me on a short tour of some of the building. "There's loads of ghosts here." Richard said as we walked towards a door marked 'Emergency Exit'. "These stairs will take us to the basement." Our footsteps echoed in the stairwell. Richard stopped on a flight of stairs. "I was showing a woman around the building one day and she stopped about here and told me that there was the spirit of a woman with us. She said that this ghost was laughing. I asked why she was laughing? The lady told me that the ghost wanted to push me down the stairs. Not in a nasty way, just in a playful way. That was a strange day. Anyway, come on, not far now." He headed off down the stairs. Soon we were deep beneath the building.

We entered the basement through a large metal door, beyond this was a warren of passageways and rooms. It was eerily quiet. I had thought there would be the noise of machinery, air conditioning or something, but it was dead quiet. "I was down here during lockdown. I had to come in and make sure that the building was locked up and safe. I was on my own, no one else in the entire building." Richard leaned over a small wall and looked down and pointed, he said "I was down there, beneath the building when it happened." I peered over the edge, below us was a much deeper part of the basement, a sub level of corridors and rooms. It was dark down there, and a cold breeze found its way up to my face, forcing me to back away. Richard must have noticed the look on my face.

"Not nice, is it?" Richard stated. I shook my head in reply. "I was down there on my own, looking around and making sure all the fire doors were shut. Then I saw someone. A shadowy figure of a towering man wearing a tall hat. He was as wide as he was tall. Just stood in the corridor. There were no lights on but I could see him. I shouted at him. 'You can't be down here', I said. Then he started to run off in the opposite direction. So, I followed him. Saw him round the corner towards a fire exit which leads to the car park outside. I turned the corner myself and he wasn't there. Must've opened the doors quick, I thought. I got to the fire doors myself and pushed them open, running out into the cold air. He was gone. There was nowhere for him to hide. He'd just vanished. Gone." Richard shook his head like he didn't believe what he'd just said.

We made our way back to the upper floors and as we walked up the stairs, he told me a horrible but true tale. It was the early 1920s, the hotel was at its height of popularity with tourists coming from around the world to visit Harrogate and stay at the Grand Hotel for its famous views across Valley Gardens. A young lady was staying on the top floor, when one evening she dressed for dinner and made her way to the lift. Pressing the button, she waited a few moments, and then without thinking pulled apart the scissor gate. She stepped inside and fell to her death. The lift had not arrived on her floor. She fell right on top of the roof of the lift and died instantly. Her ghost has been seen waiting for the lift by many visitors and guests over the centuries and people still see her even now.

Richard went on to tell me about his most terrifying experience. "I was alone at night locking up. I was walking along the corridor of floor three, when I stopped cause, I thought I heard something. It was dead quiet. I thought I must've imagined it so I carried on. But then I definitely heard something. Footsteps. Children's footsteps. They were following me, running and stopping as if we were playing a game. Well, I never agreed to play a game with no ghosts. So, I walked faster, and so did they. I ran to the door, my heart hammering in my chest and left. I never even go on that floor now. I don't mind ghosts, but ghosts of kids freak me out."

The building is known for its unusual spirit orbs.

These orbs of light have been seen in the day time and at night. Many people have reported seeing large lights floating around what used to be the ballroom.

There is also poltergeist activity which was reported to me by a security guard who had worked there on a night shift whilst they were renovating the buildings. Steve was alone in the building, working shifts with another guy who he never met. His job was to walk the building at night, check doors and windows were secure and make his presence known, so that there were signs of life inside. This was a deterrent to potential thieves. He had a room which they used as their base. There was a tea and coffee making facility, a radio, a sofa and a toilet nearby.

Steve was sat one night; he hadn't been there long when the room suddenly got cold. Looking around for an open window he found none. He didn't think much of it and settled back down to read his book. Then the room felt different, electrically charged, the hairs on his arms and neck stood on their ends. He placed his book down and surveyed the room. He felt as though something had changed, like he was no longer alone. He called out into the darkness, there was no reply. He sat back in his chair and studied the room.

He noticed the desk, on which the kettle, radio and other items were sat, had started to shake. He stood up and watched as the whole desk shuddered to life, it rocked side to side and then lifted a few inches off the ground before it landed loudly and heavily on the floor. The noise echoed throughout the empty building. Steve stood there utterly gobsmacked at what he had just witnessed. He thought for a second that there had been an earthquake but shook the silly idea from his mind. There was no explanation as to what he'd just seen other than it was something other worldly.

Weeks later Steve was walking along a corridor towards the lifts when he stopped in his tracks. Standing alone in the light of the fire exit was a woman. He called out to her but she ignored him and gave no reply. He made his way towards her apprehensively. He blinked and in that moment the girl vanished. He searched around but found no one. He was alone and scared. Steve hated the job and quit a few months in.

Paul Warner was 31 years old when he worked as a cleaner in Windsor house in 1993. On arrival, the cleaning team would meet in a small staff room, located in the basement. Paul started work just as the usual office staff would leave. He spent 90% of his time on the top floor, that was full of offices rented by the NHS.

The large octagon shaped room was carpeted and littered with desks. The office was empty. Paul had been hoovering the floor for around ten minutes when he glanced up and spotted someone wearing blue pyjamas. He assumed the figure to be a real person as it walked down the corridor where it disappeared around a corner and out of sight.

Paul was a few feet away so he took off after the person, who he assumed was a man due to his height and stature. He turned the corner and called out, expecting to see the man there but he was alone. Only a few seconds had passed between seeing the figure and going after him, so he was confused as to where the mysterious individual had gone.

Later that night, Paul was talking to a security guard about what he saw. Paul had come to the conclusion that he had just seen an office worker leaving for the night. It was then that the security guard showed him an old black and white photograph of the very same octogen room kitted out as a hospital ward. The former hotel, was requisitioned during World War One and utilised as a hospital for injured soldiers. The photograph showed some of the patients wearing the very same style of pyjamas that Paul had seen the stranger wearing earlier that evening. When Paul asked what colour the pyjamas might have been, the security guard answered "Blue. They wore blue pyjamas."

On another occasion, Paul was mopping the fire escape stairs which lead from the basement to the top floor. Incidentally, this was the very same stair case that Richard had taken me down on my visit. Paul was alone in the stairwell. He had mopped from the basement to the top floor, which left him a little breathless, even at his young age. He sat down on the top step for a moment and realised that he'd left his dustpan and brush at the very bottom. Sighing, he descended the stairs to get them.

It is fair to say that Paul had now ascended and descended the stairs once already, and in that time, no one had entered the stairwell. As he was walking back up, once again, he stopped. He could plainly hear a conversation taking place between two hushed voices. He strained his ear to listen but he couldn't make out what was being said. Paul kept up his ascent and fully expected to meet two people having a secret chat on his way up. But Paul saw nobody. He could still hear the conversation as he walked all the way back to the top of the stairs. It made no sense, he thought. Where were they?

On another occasion a member of the cleaning team was on the upper floors cleaning the NHS offices. They stopped for a moment for a rest and it was then that they heard music. Looking around for the source of the sound they saw a faint light on in a nearby office. Assuming someone had left a radio on they went to the room to turn it off. As they approached the music was clearer now. It was old fashioned, perhaps 1920s style music. They recognised it as they would often listen to this period of music whilst on holiday. When they opened the door to the office the music abruptly stopped and the light source was gone.

The building has not been fully explored for all of its hauntings and I have no doubt that more stories will come to light as time goes on.

The Cavendish Hotel

It is just a short walk up the hill of Valley Drive, overlooking Valley Gardens, to the former Cavendish Hotel. In the 1960s, two young ladies, Penny and Rose, travelled from London to Harrogate to take their secretarial exams. They had opted to share a room at the Cavendish in order to save on costs. Sleeping in separate beds, the girls settled in for the night, eager for a good night's rest ahead of their exam in the morning.

Penny's bed was nearest the large window which overlooked Valley Gardens. She woke in the middle of the night to the feeling that someone was sitting on her bed. She was right. There was someone there. "Rose? What are you doing?" she whispered. She heard another noise to her right. Turning, she was confused to see her friend fast asleep in her own bed. Penny turned back to the figure on her bed. She was ready to scream when the man stood up. Frozen in fear, her voice taken from her, she watched him and took in the details of what she saw.

The white-haired, skinny, old man looked withered and fragile as he slowly raised himself off the bed. He almost floated over to the window where he stood for a moment or two, as if enjoying the view. He then disappeared before her very eyes. Her screams woke

Rose from her slumber.

In more recent times, the same room was used as an office. One morning, the office secretary, Amanda, unlocked the door and entered the small room. There, stood in the window, was a white-haired old man. "Can I help you?" she asked. Suddenly distracted by the internal alarm beeping, she turned to punch in the pin code to disarm it. When she turned back around, the man had vanished. She searched under the two desks in the room but no one was there. She had never been able to explain this, nor had she told anyone, until she attended the Harrogate Ghost Walk in 2022.

The Crown Hotel

The Crown Hotel has a long and illustrious history dating back to 1660, when on the site, stood a small inn. Due to the influx of visitors, the hotel grew considerably in size, and by the time Lord Byron brought a bevy of ladies, dogs and horses to visit in 1806, the hotel was described as being a mini village. It was so big that it had its own farm that produced food for the guests, a blacksmith, a baker, a masonry team, a laundry unit, a large stable block and kennels for the hunting party dogs.

Much of the hotel was rebuilt in 1870 in the style you see today. The hotel sits at the heart of Harrogate's Montpellier Quarter. As you are looking at the frontage, you will note the Italian Renaissance style of the building, designed by Bristol architect J.H. Hirst. Inside, the hotel retains much of its character. A beautiful rotating door leads into a large reception area. The building is a warren of corridors and spacious, characterful rooms. The Churchill Suite is an elegant oak panelled room complete with stained glass windows and ornate ceilings.

The hotel played a role during wartime Britain and in 1939 it was requisitioned by the army and was home to the Signals Staff from RAF Leighton Buzzard. The building was given back in 1959 and returned to its use as a hotel.

The hotel has always been, and remains, popular with tourists. Over the years it has welcomed guests such as Lord Byron and Sir Edward Elgar. The hotel is so popular that some of its previous visitors refuse to leave and have taken up permanent residence.

In 2012, a female visitor from Maryland was awoken in the night to a strange rustling or scraping sound. She turned on the light to take in the room. At the foot of her bed was a small table with a chair pushed under it. There was nothing of note about the room and she was confused as to the source of the sound; she turned off the lamp and tried to go back to sleep. She was just about asleep when the scraping sound woke her again. She lay there listening, trying to pinpoint where it was coming from and who, or what could be making the noise.

She listened, it was coming from the foot of her bed, beneath it perhaps? She hurriedly switched on the lamp and turned to survey the room once more. Only this time, something was different. The chair which was, only moment ago, pushed beneath the desk, looked as though it had moved. It was pulled out from the desk by a foot or more. Or so she thought. She was tired after all and in her half wake state, she thought she had imaged it all.

Turning off the lamp, she lay her head on the pillow.

Something stopped her closing her eyes. In the silence of her room at the back of the hotel, she heard the strange noise again. Only this time, her ear was ready for the sound. It was the sound of something moving across the carpeted floor of her room. In a flash of movement, she speedily turned on the bedside lamp. So quick was she, that she was horrified to see the chair moving across the floor and coming to an abrupt halt.

Terrified that someone was in her room, beneath her bed, she called reception and begged for help. "There is someone in my room, come quick. Help." She cried down the phone.

Two female members of staff were at her door in a matter of minutes. They performed a thorough search. It was empty. The two staff members were told what had occurred. The three of them stood looking at the chair, almost afraid to touch it. The two members of staff exchanged knowing looks "It's no problem for us to move you to the front of the hotel" kindly offered one of the ladies.

"No, no it's fine. Thank you. I just need to sleep" replied the frightened guest.

She slept soundly for the rest of the night and left the hotel the next day as planned. The story usually ends there, however, one dark evening in September, a mother and daughter from Scarborough attended my ghost walk. As I regaled them with the above tale of the haunted bedroom, their faces changed from entertained to scared. They revealed that they were staying on the upper floors at the back of the hotel. The next day they had left a review of the ghost walk on my Facebook page. In it they described how they had been woken in the dead of the night to the sound of their suitcases being flung across the room.

During World War II the hotel was home to the RAF who were stationed there for a number of years. It is also said that the grand ballroom was used as a field hospital for returning members of the RAF at one stage. It should come as no surprise that the hotel has its fair share of ghosts from the war time period.

In 1991, in the early hours of the morning, at around 3:20 A.M, hotel staff member, James Venis, was performing his usual rounds. This consisted of him walking the long and peaceful corridors of the hotel, ensuring there were no issues or unwanted visitors. He moved along the soft carpet from the reception area towards the Montpellier and Byron Suites, two function rooms with ornate decoration. He opened the door to each room in turn to find the void of life. Closing the door to the Byron suite he turned and made his way down a small flight of stairs which led to the Victoria Suite.

The Victoria Suite, as it is now known, is the former grand ballroom of the hotel. A long, T-shaped room, with a bar and large carpeted area at the entrance and a stage and backstage area at the other end.

James entered the large room.

He's always felt a sense of unease in this area of the hotel. He'd worked here for around 3 years and yet still, he could not shake the feeling of dread when he entered the ballroom. He glanced to his right, in the darkness, lit only by safety lighting on a nearby fire door, he could see the outline of the stage. There were no tables or chairs, so the room felt cavernous, like a gaping mouth eager to swallow you whole.

He felt spooked, looked away and quickened his pace toward the bar. Safely behind the confines of the bar, he grabbed a glass and poured himself some water. The hum from the fridge was loud and a welcome reprieve from the eerie silence of the ballroom. He took a long gulp of water during which he heard a door open and close. The sound had clearly come from the stage end of the ballroom. James stopped drinking and lowered his glass filled hand.

He held his breath, the skin on his knuckles turned white as he clutched the glass tighter. He listened. Nothing. He placed the glass down and dared to peer over the bar and look into the dark mouth of the ballroom. He saw nothing. Just blackness. It was lighter behind the bar than in the rest of the room, so he couldn't make anything out in the dark beyond.

"Hello?" he called out. He listened. Nothing. No reply came and he silently thanked God. He stepped out from behind the bar and took a few paces across the carpeted welcome area and onto the wooden floor of the ballroom. He looked around the space and his eyes were drawn to the large windows spanning the left-hand wall of the room. James noticed that the lights that usually shone in from the courtyard and car park behind the building were not on. This meant the room was much darker than normal. The curtains were also closed which added to the thick layer of darkness in the room.

He gave himself a moment as his eyes adjusted to the obscurity of the room. Shapes started to take form, a single chair sat on the dancefloor, the stage came into view, curtains open and only more darkness beyond. As he was looking at the stage his eyes happened upon a form. It wasn't there before and yet it isn't fully there now. It was as though the dark of the room was being collected together to form a shadow. He rubbed his eyes to dispel the anomaly.

When his vision cleared a man was standing in front of him, around ten feet away. He was wearing a soldier's uniform, one that James recognised from the movies as being from World War II. James froze, the hairs on every part of his body stood on end. He could be mistaken but the man didn't seem to have a face. His face was just a shadow, but he knew there must have been a face there as the man before him was as solid and as real as he was.

"Are you staying in the hotel sir? Can I help?" There was no reply. "You can't be in here." said James sternly, hoping to scare the intruder off. There was a pause longer than James cared for and then the mysterious soldier began to move towards the exit. "You can't go through there, you'll set the fire alarm off." He knew this was a lie, the internal fire door wasn't linked to the alarm but the hotel reception would be alerted that it had been opened.

James moved towards the door too, hoping to stop the man, as he walked, he tripped on his own foot, causing him to look down briefly. He cursed and when he looked up the man had left through the door. Back at the reception, no alarm was triggered, as yet, the door had not been opened. James made haste to the fire door, he opened it and the girl at reception, Sarah, was notified by a small flashing light. Sarah made her way to the door in question.

James in the meantime was giving chase to the trespasser. Upon opening the door, he found himself in a white corridor lit by emergency lighting. He saw the man at the end of a corridor. This was a dead end; the only room down there was a locked storeroom. "Here mate, you can't be back here." called James, who had reached the turn in the corridor. He had expected to see the man trapped at the dead end, perhaps trying the door handle to the cupboard as a place to hide. There was no one there.

James assumed the cupboard was unlocked and the man was hiding inside. Just at that moment, he shot out of his skin as a woman's voice called out his name. "Jesus bloody Christ!" he bellowed. "What the hell are you doing James?" asked a bewildered Sarah, now standing by his side. James regained his composure.

"You scared the life of me. There's someone down here. A man in uniform. He's in the cupboard." James's voice had hushed tones which caused Sarah to realise the seriousness of the situation.

"Shall I call the police?" she asked.

"No. I've got him."

Sarah stayed rooted to the spot as James walked down the corridor to the cupboard. His hand darted out to the door handle and quickly turned it, this cause Sarah to jump and scream. The door handle didn't move. It was locked. He darted a confused look at Sarah. "Give me your key." She handed over the keys. James unlocked the door and found the small cupboard empty. It was full of cleaning products. The man was nowhere to be found.

James knew the history of the building and after this strange event, he and Sarah were discussing what had happened, together they decided he had seen the ghost of a soldier from the RAF.

This isn't the only sighting of a soldier in the hotel, there have been a number of reports of men in uniform walking around in the dead of night. A friend of mine, Gareth, who co-runs 'Dead Northern', a fantastic, horror film festival, has had his own experience too. We discussed it over a beer and BBQ at his house, as our wives talked and our children played together.

"I was there to see my mate, Rick." Gareth took a sip from his cold beer. "Rick is always doing events around Harrogate and he was setting up for the beer festival hosted by the Harrogate Round Table. I'd asked someone where Rick was and they told me he was on the stage. I went into the Victoria Suite and saw it was empty. I called out for Rick, but no one answered. It was then I saw him on the stage, just walking across from one side to the other. I made my way to the stage, calling his name as I went. He just ignored me, which was weird. Anyway, when I got to the stage there was no one there. I climbed up and checked backstage but it was empty. Rick was gone. Whomever I had seen had vanished." He turned over the burgers which were sizzling on the BBQ.

"And you think you saw a ghost?" I asked.

"I don't know to be honest. There was definitely someone there. I couldn't make out what they were wearing, and in hindsight, they were the wrong height and body shape to be Rick. But I was expecting to see Rick on the stage, so perhaps my mind thought it was going to see someone up there. When I looked at the stage at first it was empty, but then I saw a figure walking across. Maybe my brain made me see something which it was expecting to see if that makes sense?" Gareth believes in the spirit world but I liked the way he was thinking. He wanted to explain the situation rationally and maybe he had. Maybe his brain had played a trick on him or possibly, it was something paranormal.

A former manager of the hotel told a story about a ghost he witnessed on the second floor. One evening in the dead of night, the manager was walking the hallways of the first floor. He was stopped in his tracks when he spotted a young boy playing with a ball in a corridor. The boy was up late he thought as he looked at the time on his watch, but when he looked up the boy had vanished.

The Churchill suite is the main dining room for the hotel. One quiet afternoon a couple had just finished their meal, there were only a few of other guests dotted around at various tables. Looking up, the husband spotted a waiter standing idle in the corner of the room some distance away. 'Excuse me, please could we have the bill?' he called across the room. The waiter ignored him. After a short pause he said 'Please can we have the bill?'

'Perhaps he can't hear you love.' said his wife.

The man got up and started to walk over to the member of staff. Only when he looked again the staff member had vanished. He looked around and saw no one. Later, as he was complaining to management about the incident, he was asked to describe the staff member in question. He described a young man wearing an odd-looking uniform. The manager informed him that members of their staff wore simple black trousers and a white shirt with a name tag. This was clearly not a member of the hotel's team.

There are further stories of the waiter who has been seen standing idly in the corner of the Churchill suite. Other members of staff call out to him, thinking he is real, only for him to vanish. The basement holds tales of unusual activity but no one has been brave enough to come forward with their secrets.

I love the Crown Hotel; the history and character are second to none and they are proud of their ghostly heritage and like to share their stories. They have helped me out a great deal and continue to support me in my business ventures. I host a number of events there, from paranormal nights, ghost hunts in their haunted basement, to Halloween shows. My friend Neil Bradley-Smith and I are their resident mind reader and magician where we host a monthly show together.

The Cairn Hotel

A mid-nineteenth century former Victorian house that dominates the landscape of Harrogate like a sinister castle. Set in lovely gardens on the south side of town and once home to a local vicar, it is a stunning property, heavily extended over time with stained glass windows, fine architecture and period features throughout.

It was built by A. E. Harter Esq as a home for himself and his family. It came with extensive landscaped gardens, tennis courts, stables, a coach house and a luxurious interior. It was sold to The Duchy of Lancaster which still owns it to this day.

Just over a year after it was bought, catastrophe struck. The east wing was devastated by a fire that occurred when a servant ignited a curtain with a candle. Is it not strange then, that history should repeat itself but with tragic consequences? In May 2010, a fire ripped through the staff quarters at the hotel. Guests and staff fled the building but sadly, a man who worked in the kitchens was found dead.

In the 1800s, the building was already in use as a hotel but under the name 'The Cairn Hydro Hotel.' The hotel still has the original spring water fed baths that are sadly not in use today.

The gardens, although smaller than they were in the

Victorian era, are said to be haunted by the sound of children laughing, crying and screaming in horror. It is rumoured that at least one child died on the grounds during the Victorian era.

Many guests and staff have complained about the feeling of the utmost dread and terror in the main toilets of the hotel. Nothing has ever been seen but the feeling of fear seems to grip you when you are in this area.

I visited the hotel in July 2022 where I was meeting with Chris Myers, the founder of North Yorkshire Paranormal Investigators (NYPI). Chris is a multitalented man. When I arrived, he was nearing the end of his set, playing the guitar, banjo and keyboard with energy and skill. He is employed by the hotel to serenade the guests and he does it very well indeed.

After his set had finished, I was introduced to his team and we had a short discussion about the spirit world. They were all very welcoming and each had their own theories about it all. I shared my theory that I believed the power of the water beneath Harrogate supplied the spirit world with energy, enough to continue their hauntings and manifestations. This began a new discussion about just this topic. I don't know if it was all the talk of water, but I needed to use the facilities. Chris pointed to an old metal door behind me I followed the signs to the men's cloakroom.

There were two flights of stairs leading down to the

basement area of the hotel. Upon reaching the second flight, I paused, the hairs on my arms stood on their end and my skin was awash with goosepimples. The air felt different here, electrically charged. I honestly felt as though there was someone else there. "Hello?" I called out. No answer. Phew! I reached the bottom of the stairs, to my right were another set of stairs leading downwards into pitch black. To my left was an open door and stepping through it I could hear the sound of rushing water. 'Must be the toilets' I thought. I opened the door and was hit in the face by heat and steam.

To the right is a row of sinks and taps, with a mirror running the entire length of the wall. The mirror was completely steamed up, the culprit was a hot tap which was turned on fully and water was gushing out of it and into the sink. It must have been on a long time I thought as I moved to turn the tap off. Only as I turned the tap, the water wouldn't stop. So, I turned the other tap and still, nothing happened. I stepped forwards even more and stepped into water. Looking down the floor was completely covered in water. I looked around the corner to the cubicles and urinals and the entire floor area was about 3 cm deep in water. 'Must have been going for hours' I thought to myself. I turned back to the tap and tried again. Turning the taps had no effect. I do not know why, but I said out loud, "Please just let me turn the tap off now." I tried again and low and behold the water stopped.

I surveyed the scene. There was an open window at the end of the room, outside of which was an area accessible from the gardens. So rationally, someone could have got in here and purposefully turned the tap on. Perhaps some kids were set on causing damage, or one of the guests had the same trouble as I had and couldn't turn the tap off, simply left it running, not thinking it would flood.

I looked back to the sink to find that the water had not spilled over the sink edge like I had assumed. I wasn't sure how the floor had become so flooded. I rushed upstairs and told a member of staff that the toilets were flooded, he looked confused and made his way downstairs.

Chris overheard what I had said and followed him, I stayed close behind them. When Chris got to the same stairs where I had previously felt the hairs raise on my arms, he stopped. Turning to me he said "I feel something here. A presence. It is very active tonight." It could have been a coincidence that he stopped where I had felt something, but who knows?

We all went into the men's cloakroom. A manger was now with us. "What happened do you think?" I asked.

"Some guest might have not been able to turn the tap off. Just left it, probably. I'll get someone to mop this up." And he left.

I told Chris about my experience on the stairs, he agreed that he had felt something at the same place. We left the room discussing what had happened. In all honesty I don't know what to make of it. It could have just been some hapless guest, most of which were over 60, but I doubt any of them would simply leave a tap running on purpose. They could have forgotten to turn it off I suppose. Or was this a sign from the many spirits that seem to haunt the hotel? Perhaps they were showing me that my theory about spirits using water was indeed true.

I had just been discussing this very subject prior to my watery discovery. But then, when something unusual happens we tend to lean toward the paranormal, especially if you are that way inclined in your beliefs. I don't know what or who was responsible for the flood, but it undoubtedly made me consider a more paranormal answer.

There is one ghost who has plagued staff and is the rumoured cause of many housekeepers fleeing the building. It resides in one of the bedrooms on the upper floors.

In the corner of the hotel is a dark room, it should be bathed in light and sun as it is lucky enough to have large windows overlooking the grounds, yet it is always dark - dark and cold. So cold in fact, that after a number of complaints from guests, the radiators were turned up to full. Still the room was, by all accounts, freezing. Management then brought in standalone heaters, but they did little to raise the temperature.

The constant cold in the room has left many people baffled, for the coldness in the room seems to emanate from the floor, and it is here where our ghost is seen.

One rainy afternoon, Vicky, a housekeeper, was walking down a long corridor to the room in question. A moment earlier, her colleague had asked her to go and clean this particular room, even though it was not on Vicky's list of rooms to clean.

"It's on your floor, isn't it?" asked Vicky.

"Yeah, but newbies have to do as they're told." joked her colleague. Vicky had not long been working at the hotel. She had been looking for work for a long time, so she was happy to do whatever to keep her job. "Fine, give me the key and I'll go clean it." She walked off to her colleagues laughing and joking about something she had clearly missed.

She placed the key in the lock and turned it, opening in the door she was hit in the face by a blast of ice-cold air, every hair stood on end, goose skin crept over her flesh; she froze in abject horror. On the floor was a young girl in a long, old-fashioned brown dress. The girl was solid and she was furiously scrubbing away at the floor, brush in hand, bucket by her side. "Hello?"

whispered a petrified Vicky.

The girl stopped cleaning, turned to face Vicky, and let out the most horrific scream. Vicky ran screaming from the room, down the stairs, out of the front door and never went back there again.

The ghost of the cleaning girl continues to torture staff to this day.

The Cedar Court Hotel

The building has stood on the same site since 1672, although it has changed internally many times. It was a hospital in 1959 and a base for soldiers during WWII. The hotel as it stands today is a rambling three storey building; it blends modern hotel luxuries with fantastically preserved period features.

The hotel is stunning both inside and out, and overlooks the 200 acres Stray parkland. The elegant frontage is handsome, with arched sash bay windows which climb full height up the building. Inside are a number of function rooms, including the grand ballroom with original cornices and Tuscan style columns throughout.

The hotel, with its numerous uses over the centuries, has collected a number of interesting and fantastical hauntings. Over the years there have been many, many sightings of ladies in Victorian dress, some of which make for amazing stories.

Once, a handyperson, Wilfred, or Wilf as he's best known, was tasked with fixing some electrics in a function room. Wilf had worked at the hotel many times in the past. He was as Yorkshire as they come and has no belief in ghosts or anything paranormal whatsoever. He got to the room in questions and, upon opening the door, was surprised to see the room filled with gossiping ladies in what he assumed were fancy dress costumes, sitting on chairs drinking tea, some standing chatting.

He apologised, closed the doors and turned to leave when a young member of staff, named Ryan, asked what he was doing. "Supposed to be working in there but the room's full of ladies having a tea party or something." Wilf said, slightly bewildered.

"There's no one in there. Not today." Replied Ryan as he opened the doors to the room to reveal it was completely empty. Wilf, tentatively took two steps into the room. His jaw hung open; the blood rushed out of his face. "Where the bloody hell did they all go?" He mumbled in utter disbelief. Ryan had no answer for him.

Over the years many guests have reported similar sightings of ladies in old clothing. One evening in 1989, Simon and Samantha returned to the hotel having enjoyed a meal in town. It was gone 11:45 P.M. The hotel was quiet, one or two guests were enjoying a night cap in the lobby.

Simon and Sam were tired and headed to their hotel suite. They stood outside their room, placed the key in the lock and opened the door. To their shock, the room was filled with sunlight, even though it was pitch dark outside. It took a moment for their eyes to adjust to the sudden onslaught of the sun's rays. When their vision returned, they saw two ladies sitting on chairs in front of the window drinking tea at a little table. The women were elegantly dressed in large flowing dresses. They paid no attention to the couple, as they sat drinking tea from small cups, saucer held beneath to catch any drips. They smiled as they drank, bathed in sunlight which poured in from the window.

The couple apologised profusely and quickly shut the door. They both stared at each other in total bewilderment. "I thought this was our room?" said Simon as he looked down at the key in his hand, a little plastic key ring with the number 36 looked back at him. His gaze went to the number on the door which also read 36. "This is our room." He whispered. Sam, took the key from his hand and double checked. She looked around them, the corridor was certainly familiar "There must be some mistake." She knocked on the door and waited. No one came to answer. She knocked again "Hello?" She raised her voice. Nothing. Simon took hold of the door handle "We're coming in, I think there's been some sort of mistake."

He opened the door and was immediately struck by a cold draught, that and the fact the room was in complete darkness. He fumbled for the light switch, finding it, he flipped it up. The room was empty and dark. The once open curtains were now closed, the table and chairs the two ladies were sat at had evaporated and the women themselves had all but disappeared.

"What the hell?" exclaimed Simon, he opened the bathroom door anticipating the ladies would be hiding inside. It was empty. Sam dashed to the closed curtains and pulled them open with force, half expecting to find the ladies there. Nothing. "Why was it so light in here a moment ago?" asked Simon as he sat on the bed absolutely confused. Sam just stood there, her head shaking in all-embracing disbelief. "What just happened?" she eventually managed.

"God knows." Was all Simon could muster.

The numerous sightings of Victorian ladies strike me as somewhat unusual. I mean, seeing a ghost is an unusual experience, I can vouch for that. The way in which many people have experienced these Victorian ladies at this hotel has been described as though the witness were stepping back in time. Not that they were seeing a ghost. Simply that they had gone back to the past and were witnessing a very specific moment in time replaying. It is very rare for furniture to be part of a haunting. Both the handyman and the couple had seen chairs, tables, teacups and saucers which is highly unusual. The above tale even had sunlight in the apparent haunting, even though it was the middle of the night.

These stories continue into the modern day. In 2014, a guest returned to their room to find a man dressed in a suit. The guest chased the man out who promptly disappeared down a corridor. The hotel staff checked the locks of the door, they had not been forced open, the man had not gained entry via any of the closed and locked windows. No one knows how he got in or who he was.

The attic lies abandoned, used mainly for storage, and is a place many of the staff dare not visit alone. A number of staff members have reported the smell of tobacco smoke up there. There have also been sightings of two- or three-men wearing WWII uniforms standing nearby a window, smoking and appearing to talk. These gentlemen may be remnants from the time the hotel was requisitioned by the army during WWII.

A friendly, naughty, and affectionately named Mable, is a ghost said to be that of a chambermaid who passed away nearly 200 years ago. Mable is a most useful spirit in that she likes to clean rooms, particularly the bathrooms. She is also responsible for the name of 'the spooky corridor'. For it is here where she likes to scare staff, move objects and occasionally trip people over.

The Old Swan Hotel

In 1777, the Swan Inn was situated in what was known as the settlement, Low Harrogate. Come the 19th Century, it was redeveloped by the Harrogate Hydropathic Company and began a new life as a fashionable spa hotel which included its very own Turkish baths. Known as The Harrogate Hydro, it even had its own farm on Penny Pot Lane which provided its own source of locally grown food for the kitchens. In 1939, the hotel was amongst many others which was requisitioned, with a mere forty-eight hours' notice, by the Ministry of Aircraft Production. The German military found out about the building's use and attacked it with enemy aircraft in 1943. There were three bombs on the plane. The first levelled an empty property at the end of Swan Road, the next bomb landed in the grounds of the Majestic Hotel and the third went straight through the occupied hotel roof of the Majestic, though fortunately did not explode.

In December of 1926, the hotel was at the centre of the disappearance of author Agatha Christie, who had vanished from her home in Berkshire. Over the course of the next 11 days, one of the largest manhunts ever mounted at the time ensued to find the missing writer. More than one thousand policemen alongside hundreds of civilians and, for the first time, aeroplanes were involved to find Agatha. Even Sir Arthur Conan Doyle was involved in the search whereby he consulted with a clairvoyant who claimed that the missing lady would be found alive and near water. Had he only thought to revisit the spa town of Harrogate, he would have found Agatha enjoying the delights of Swan Hydropathic Hotel, under the assumed name of Mrs Teresa Neele (the name of her husband's mistress.) It was an unassuming banjo player, playing at the hotel, who recognised her and brought the manhunt to an abrupt end. The Grade II listed building has seen many people pass through its doors and remains today a much-loved hotel. But there are some guests and employees who remain within its walls.

There is part of the hotel, which guests will never see, shrouded in mystery. There are a large proportion of rooms and corridors which are closed off to staff and guests. This collection of rooms comprises of the old staff accommodation, various storage rooms, and offices, all of which lie behind locked doors, littered with remnants from the past and covered in a thick layer of ancient dust. I cannot, at the time of writing, find any information as to why these rooms are all derelict but having spoken to some past employees, I have formed my own theory. They are haunted. So haunted, in fact, that the best way to manage the manifestations is to shut the area off to use. That's just my theory, though it's backed by the following accounts.

Christopher Emery was twenty-four years old when he worked at the Swan Hotel in 2012. We sit together having a drink, he is thirty-four now and his experiences during his time at the Swan changed him forever. His first encounter with a ghost was as a young 16-year-old. Chris was staying at his friend's house, a 100-year-old farmhouse in Dallowgill which was a small village to the West of Ripon. The house was old, full of character and was situated in the middle of the moors. Chris had heard his friend's family tell of how the home was haunted but he had never been told any specific stories. He did not care to hear them, not that he did or didn't believe, he just wasn't interested. His view was about to change forever.

Chris had stayed at his friend's house many times in his youth but one night was much different to the rest. He was staying in a new part of the house, an annex, built onto the end of the kitchen. His sofa bed rested against the far wall of the room. He was just getting comfortable when he heard some strange noises coming from the open kitchen door. His clear view from his bed saw through the kitchen and onto the set of stairs at the end of a long hallway. It was an ominous view and a cold shiver ran up his spine. The noises came again and, as he listened, he imagined a family cat making its way across the kitchen worktop, clattering some left-over cutlery against dirty plates from their tea.

Only, the family didn't have a cat. Yet the noise was there, sounding like metal against glass, a light but audible tinkering sound. Chris saw a young girl, with blonde hair and dressed in a white nightgown, walk right past the door nearest to him. As she made her way past him, she turned her head slightly and took a glimpse of where Chris lay, looking straight at him. He felt a wave of excitement wash over him. Adrenaline pumping, he said out loud, "Woah! What the hell?" He quickly got out of bed and ran to the doorway. He looked to the right, where she should be, only she wasn't there. The front door was a few feet away. It was locked and he hadn't heard it open. "That was a ghost," he said out loud. As Chris told me his story, I could sense that he almost felt privileged to have seen the manifestation of the little girl. As a 16-year-old, he felt excited and confused by it. By the time he was an adult, he had left the experience behind him and had almost all but forgotten about it. That was until he started working at The Old Swan Hotel.

The now 24-year-old Chris was on a journey to follow his ambitions to become a head chef. He started at The Old Swan as a kitchen assistant, eventually working his way up to chef de partie. As a kitchen assistant, he was responsible for the breakfast sitting and was part of a skeleton team consisting of a breakfast supervisor and a night porter. As Chris walked towards the hotel, the thin drizzle that had soaked him through stopped. Typical, he thought to himself. He got to the back door where the night porter was smoking a cigarette. They greeted each other and Chris went inside. He usually went straight up to the staff area where he would remove his coat and change into his work attire but he thought differently this day and decided to get straight on with some work.

Switching on the lights, he took everything in. The kitchens were kitted out with all the modern facilities but the architecture was from the 1900s. Some of the other chefs thought that the place could do with a bit of modernising but Chris admired and liked the old building. He opened the fridge and began removing various trays of pre-cooked food for breakfast. He noticed that some lazy git had not bothered to cut the tomatoes in half, so he set about the task.

After placing a board on the counter, knife in hand, he started cutting. In front of Chris was a doorway without a door. It had always been like this. It gave you a clear view down a T-junction corridor, with the top of the T closest to the door. The hallway led from right to left. To the left was a small flight of stairs which led to the old staff accommodation area. There was only one room in use in this part of the hotel; the staff changing room. All of the other passageways and rooms were closed off and never used. They always held an air of mystery about them for Chris. Why was this part of the hotel left to rot and ruin? What was behind all of those locked doors?

Chris was absently thinking about this when he heard a heavy set of footsteps fast approaching the opening in front of him. The steps got louder when suddenly a man pelted past the doorway heading towards the staff area. In that moment, Chris caught a glimpse of him. He was wearing a long, dark green, army-type jacket or rain mac and perhaps a black beanie-style hat, though he ran so fast past him that he could have been mistaken.

Chris thought, who the bloody hell is that at this time in the morning? Realising that he didn't recognise the man as a member of staff, and knowing no guests should be down there, he assumed he was an intruder, perhaps running away from someone. "Oi!" he shouted after the man. Chris stepped forward a couple of feet and was in the corridor. Looking left he saw the man who was about to ascend the stairs but he was running so fast that he slipped and fell. He landed hands first with a thud and he let out a "Humph!" as he hit the stairs awkwardly.

"Are you alright mate?" he called. The man, ignoring Chris' concern, was quick to regain his composure and carried on running up the stairs. "You shouldn't be down here. Get back!" he shouted as he flipped on the light switch and gave chase after the intruder. He reached the top of the stairs and it was quiet. He could no longer hear the man's footsteps. "Hello?" he called out. Chris opened the door to the shower rooms, which no one ever used, and it was empty. He checked in the staff room, where he would usually have been by now getting changed into his uniform had he not decided to start work straight away. It too was empty. There were only locked doors left to check but he was beginning to feel a bit sick, scared almost of what had just happened. This part of the building had always felt creepy but now, after this, he felt like he didn't want to be there. He hurriedly made his way back to the kitchen.

Shaken, he decided not to change in the staff room, but instead dressed into his uniform in the back of the kitchen. He then popped outside for some fresh air. There he found Eddy the night porter. "Eddy. I think I've just seen a ghost."

Eddy nodded, "Aye, you wouldn't be the first. There're lots of people that's seen ghosts here."

Chris continued, "He ran past me, along the corridor that goes to the staff room and then he disappeared."

"That'd be right. He's been seen up there by lots of people," said Eddy, before he walked off back to work.

Later on in the shift, the other chefs arrived. He told them of his experience and while some laughed it off, others said, "Oh aye, there's a load of ghosts here," but one of the chefs he was closer to took more of an interest. Chris re-enacted the whole experience again for his friend. Almost trying to make sense of it for himself, Chris walked him through the entire story.

They eventually ended up in the corridor where all of the locked rooms were, beyond the staff room. "He couldn't have gone in any of these rooms, they're all locked, right?" suggested Chris.

"I dunno. Let's try them all," said his friend, curiosity growing in his voice. And they did. Every door was locked but the last. Chris heaved at the door and it opened. The two chefs were hit with the overwhelming, musty smell of damp. They took in the empty, small box room with its one window, sunlight pouring through now the morning's rain had passed, seemingly revealing nothing. Typical, thought Chris.

The sunlight picked up particles of dust which seemed to dance to silent music. Chris looked around. A thick layer of dust covered everything but then something he would never have expected to see was there. Sat on the dusty old table was a beautifully fresh, bright-looking orange. There was no dust on it, it was not rotten, and it was as fresh as if someone had just placed it here seconds before. Chris looked at his friend. They both shuddered, closed the door and never returned. Chris tried not to think too much about the orange and how odd it was for it just to be sat there on a desk in an unused room. When he did, he just thought it was the oddest thing he had ever seen.

One night, Chris stood in the kitchen with the Polish kitchen porter, Tomek. They were both absently playing on their phones out of boredom when, all of a sudden, a loud crash caused them to turn around. They saw a pile of metal trays falling from a rack of shelves and sliding across the floor. Tomek stood and made the sign of the cross, hoping for protection from his faith. This incident would appear at first to be a simple accident waiting to happen. Had someone stacked the trays haphazardly? Then they may have eventually fallen due to their own weight. Tomek was convinced it was the action of a ghost.

Tomek was living on-site in the staff accommodation. Once, when he was alone in his room with the door and windows shut, the curtains began billowing and blowing as if a strong wind had found its way in. He sat up in his bed, made the sign of the cross and ran out. He made his way to reception and demanded to be moved to another room or else he would quit his job. He was moved rooms that very night without question.

Behind the scenes of the hotel is not the only place that is haunted. The main part of the hotel also has its fair share of activity. One evening, a couple who were staying in the hotel was short on towels for their room. The husband decided to go to reception and request some more. Opening the door and stepping into the corridor he saw a member of staff pushing a trolly in front of him. "Excuse me, please could we get some more towels for our room, we seem to be short?" asked the guest politely. The member of staff simply ignored the request and carried on walking away. "Excuse me? Did you hear me?" called the guest after him, but the staff member carried on, walking around a corner out of sight. Angered by the rudeness of the hotel staff member, the guest made his way to reception to complain.

"What did he look like?" asked the apologetic receptionist.

"He was old, maybe in his seventies or eighties. He was wearing a blue jacket with lapels on his shoulders, silver buttons on them and a funny looking hat." The receptionist stared at the customer. "I'm sorry Sir. He wasn't one of our staff. We don't have anyone of that description working here. No one has worn that type of uniform since the 1920s." The guest looked back at her in disbelief.

"So what? I've just seen a ghost?" he asked, incredulously.

"We will send some towels up to you sir."

This is not the only account of the ghostly porter at the hotel. Other guests and staff have also spotted the old man pushing a trolley silently down the same hallway.

One evening, a porter was alone in the ballroom, cleaning. He stopped working as he heard two people having a hushed conversation on the stage. He made his way to the stage area and could clearly hear, from the tones of voice, a secretive conversation taking place. He climbed the stage, eager to listen, but he found it to be deserted.

The strangest account from The Old Swan Hotel comes from a lady who once worked there in the late 1990s. For the purposes of discretion, we shall call her Lisa. Back then, the dilapidated staff area, where Chris had his terrifying experience, was still in use. There were a number of private accommodation rooms in the hotel with a bed and side table, even a wardrobe if you were lucky. The rooms were small, cramped and, as such, the bathroom was separate. Down the hall were the showers. Lisa had a number of unexplainable experiences in the staff accommodation area but one stood out as being the most disturbing of them all.

One night, after a long shift, Lisa was in the bathroom. Alone in the locked room, she turned on the shower, undressed and stepped into the small cubicle. The wooden door had a gap at the base, about a foot high. She was in the middle of her shower when she suddenly felt cold, even though the water was still warm. She turned the knobs, trying in vain to make the water hotter. Looking down to the floor, she could see the toes of a pair of black boots. Whoever was wearing them must have been standing with their face close to the door. Lisa began screaming for help but the feet didn't move. She began screaming obscenities at the person on the other side of the door in the hope that it would scare them off. Dread took hold and Lisa thought something terrible was about to happen to her. Then the feet were gone. She kept on shouting for help but no one came to her aid. She eventually opened the cubicle door to find the room was empty and the main door was still locked. Could the feet have belonged to the same man that Chris had seen years later? Both were wearing black boots and were seen in the exact same part of the hotel, only years apart.

The Alexandra

Now known locally as The Alex, the building was previously known as The Albion Hotel, dating back to 1840. It was re-named as The Alexandra in 1899 and once featured grand lounges, smoking rooms and a stable to the rear. It sits in a prime position overlooking the Stray parkland.

It is one of the 25 hotels requisitioned for military usage during WWII when it was used as a boarding house for RAF pilots. Original propaganda posters are still displayed in the pub. In fact, the upper floors of the building still hold artefacts and objects from the war time era. These include an un-opened safe, posters, metal sprung hospital beds, chairs, tables and former RAF soldiers. The latter being those of the ghostly variety.

The Alexandra is made up of six floors including the basement. To my knowledge, the top three floors have been abandoned to time. They lay wasted and ruined, ravaged by the elements. Pigeons are the only living creatures one will find here. These floors are said to be some of the most haunted parts of the building.

The Alexandra lays claim to some of the most extraordinary CCTV I have ever seen of actual poltergeist activity. One evening in October 2016, a video was posted to their Facebook page. It is still there today and offers a first-hand look at the poltergeist activity which takes place at the bar. In the video, you will see CCTV footage overlooking a till, the pub is closed and empty for the night. At the bottom left-hand side of the screen is a shelf with glasses sitting on it. About 20 seconds in, the emergency lights flicker on and off for no reason. Then shortly afterwards, a large wine glass falls bottom over mouth a number of times before smashing on the floor. No one can account for how this happened.

This is not the only unusual activity which takes place. The oddest paranormal activity resides in the darkest part of the building, the basement.

One staff member described the following, "I don't like it down there. There's an abnormal, ominous feeling in the basement." Gillon was stood behind the bar, eyes darting left to right, ready to serve anyone who wanted to order a drink. He appeared nervous. "I was down there a few months ago. I got to the bottom of the stairs and there was this, I don't know. This blob of light floating around." Gillon struggled to find the right words.

"What did it look like?" I probed.

"It was a ball of light, just hovering, but it had mass to it, you know what I mean? Like it was alive, moving. Like a ball of snot with a light inside. Sounds daft I know, but it's the only way I can describe it." He shook his head almost as if he didn't believe his own story.

"You'll think I'm nuts, do you?" He asked.

"I don't mate. You wouldn't believe some of the stories I've heard." I replied. "What happened next then?" I wanted to hear more.

"I ran out of there is what happened. I didn't tell anyone 'cause I was embarrassed. Who'd have believed me anyway?" A man approached the bar. "I better..." He walked off to deal with the customer.

Gillon is not the only person to see unusual orbs of light in the basement of The Alexandra. Other staff came forward with similar, if not exacting tales, of strange globules of floating light. These are what I believe are spirit orbs, the most basic form of spiritual energy.

The upper floors of the pub are some of the most active parts of the building. Perhaps this is why these floors have been left to wrack and ruin. On my ghost walk, each night we stop across the road from the Alex and I ask my guests to look up at the building and tell me what is wrong with it. Most guess correctly, that the upper floors seem bereft of life, empty and unused. The upper stories of the building are indeed unused but not empty.

As mentioned previously, there is a wealth of WWII paraphernalia up there, in fact, if you explore the walls of the bar on the main floor, you will find WWII posters and documents on display, rescued from the rooms above. Perhaps this is why soldiers have been seen lurking around these dark and dusty floors, for some spirits form an attachment to objects from their time period.

In the early 1970s, Marcus was working as a manager at the hotel. He actually lived on the first floor for a short while. His bedroom was at the front of the building and he remembered it was deathly quiet at night.

We were talking over a video call, his voice was hoarse from years of smoking, even though he'd quit, you could hear the rasping in his words, "You could hear a pin drop at night. It was a peculiar kind of quiet. You'd expect there to be some sort of noise from the building, you know, creaking and the like but it was as though the building had no life." Marcus paused and took a sip of water before continuing without interruption.

"Anyway, one night I was about ready for bed when I heard a noise. Usually wouldn't have bothered me, but as it was always quiet, this stood out. It came from above somewhere. It was a scraping, squeaking noise, like something being dragged across the wooden floor. I stopped to listen. There it was again. Like a chair being pulled from beneath a table. That's what I imagined. But it was far off, you know, distant. I'd been there for a good few months and it wasn't a sound I recognised, so, I went to investigate. I grabbed my keys and headed to the next floor above. I'd not been up here before. I was told it was derelict, not worth going up there. The door was locked, in fact every door to every floor was locked when I got to it. I followed the sound all the way to the top floor. It was eerily quiet. I could see that everything was covered in a thick layer of dust.

"There were these WWII posters on the wall, 'Your country needs you' and stuff like that. There were metal beds, tables and chairs and the like. I stood listening for a while. After about five minutes, I heard something at the far end of this long hallway. So, I followed the sound. It led me to a chair which sat ominously at the end of the corridor. It looked out of place. Just sat facing the window which had amazing views onto the Stray."

He continued to tell me how he had approached the chair and noted that there were no signs of anyone having been up there for years. He said the dust was thick and only his footprints could be seen. To his left was an archway which opened into a room that held a table, surrounded by three chairs. Yet where you'd assume the fourth chair to be, were four small indents in the dust.

"I looked at the chair sat alone in the window. I lifted it up, dust and debris fell from it. I placed it gently down and the four legs fitted perfectly into the four indents in the dust. Then I left." The next night, at around the same time, the same sound came from up there. Marcus said he rushed up only to find the chair back in the same window.

"I scanned the floor looking for another set of prints but there was just mine. Who the hell had moved the chair, I thought? I moved it back beneath the table, convinced now that this is where it was meant to be, and I went back to bed. Next night, I was waiting on the floor below. Thought I would catch the culprit who was playing a trick on me. I was certain that someone was using the old service lift to get up there and move the chair. I sat on an old sofa just waiting. Nearly nodded off when I heard the sound. I rushed up the stairs and got to the corridor to find I was alone, looking at the same chair in the same spot. I checked the service lift, it was still on the lower floors, not moved at all, probably not for years. I left the chair where it was. And do you know what? I never heard it move again after that. I always fancied going up there and removing the chair altogether. See what would happen. But I never did. Some of the staff think there is the ghost of a solider who sits on the chair. You know, looking out of the window at the view. All I know is that it baffled me then and it does to this day."

Marcus went on to tell me about a number of other strange occurrences, one of which he doesn't want me to include in this book. He told me the story and I only wish he'd allow me to include it as it is unbelievable. He was more than happy for me to include it in my ghost walk, so if you are ever in Harrogate then please join me and you can hear the unusual story first hand. I asked why he didn't want it featured in the book. His reply was that "People will think I'm making it up or that I'm off my trolley."

The Alex remains an oddity to me. The forsaken upper floors are rife for development and could make the owners a pretty penny too. However, for whatever reason, they remain to this day, abandoned and uninhabited. I wholly believe that these empty rooms are affected by the stone tape theory. Moments in time keep repeating themselves, over and over again. The WWII objects that remain up there allow the spirits attached to them to keep going. Acting out moments from their lived lives.

It's a melancholy thought to think that a soldier is sitting in a chair overlooking the Stray for all eternity. So, if you pass by the Alex, look up to the upper windows and give a little wave to the soldier in the window.

The Granby Care Home -
Formerly The Granby Hotel

Located on the edge of The Stray, The Granby Care Home offers fantastic views, easy access to town and an array of hauntings and unusual activity. The eighteenth-century former Granby Hotel stands on the site of two previous inns. The first was built in 1607 and was originally called 'The Sinking Ship', later being renamed 'The Royal Oak'.

The building you see today has been known as the Granby Hotel since 1795. In the late 18th Century through to the 19th Century, when the wells of high Harrogate were at their most visited, it was one of the premier hotels in the North of England. The hotel was popular with royalty, Robert Clive, also known as 1st Baron Clive and Clive of India, stayed here.

The hotel boasted comfortably furnished bedrooms with hot and cold water, many with private bathrooms and even telephones. Each room came with its very own gas fire.

In their beautifully decorated restaurant, you could enjoy a trio playing the latest music whilst you dined on their finest cuisine. They even possessed a garage and petrol pump, should one need to fill their tank.

Due to its location on the outskirts of town, the hotel fell into demise after the Second World War. It was refurbished and turned into the care home you see today.

Inside, it preserves much of its character, including the stunning Crystal Ballroom, sash windows, and balconies. It also retains some of its past staff including the ghost of a servant who many have witnessed and is home to a lot of poltergeist activity.

The top floor of the building is reputed to be very haunted. If you were to drive past on any given evening, you will notice the distinct lack of lights on the top floor. Very few people ever visit this part of the building, and although there are some residents up there, much of it is used for storage or offices.

It just so happens that in one of the windows on this floor, many people have witnessed a young girl wearing old fashioned clothing sitting in a window, staring out over The Stray. It is believed that she was once a maid who worked at the Granby Hotel. There are even rumours she was murdered, but I have yet to find any evidence of this during my research. Perhaps though, the apparition is responsible for the poltergeist activity which has been reported by many staff members who have worked at the care home over the years.

It was 1993 and Tracy Parker was 22 years old. She had worked at the care home for a couple of months now and was enjoying her time there. She got on well with her team mates and she loved caring for the residents.

However, she didn't love the top floor of the care home. One night a resident called down to reception and Tracy was asked to take a look in on them. They had reported that someone was in their room. Upon entering the ladies' room, Tracy noticed a foul smell. She put her hand to her nose and made her way to open a window. "It's no use Tracy" said the resident who was sat in a chair in the corner of the room. "You can't get rid of the smell. It'll soon be gone though." Tracy still opened the nearest window; as she was doing so, she replied "Agnes, you said someone was in your room?" Agnes sighed.

"You won't believe me." Tracy sat on the edge of the bed.

"Try me."

"Well, I was sat here, as I do every night and in came this woman. Bold as brass she was. Walked straight through the door." She shook her head in disbelief.

"Why was your door open?" asked Tracy.

"Oh no love. The door was shut. That's what I mean, she walked through the door." Agnes emphasised.

"Oh, right." Tracy's reply was short which led Agnes to say,

"See, I told you. No way you'd believe me. She walked right through that door there. She came up to my wardrobe, stood there for a moment and then she vanished. She's been doing that for months, and I'm sick of it. Complained to my son, told him to tell you lot but he didn't believe me. So, nothing's been done about her." Tracy didn't know what to think.

"What did she look like Agnes?" Agnes thought for a moment.

"She has on a white dress and a silly hat, like the chefs wear." Agnes answered.

Tracy listened to Agnes and as she did, she noticed the smell had gone just like Agnes said it would. Tracy put the smell down to bodily functions and thought nothing more of it. Tracy left Agnes to sleep, and said she would check on her in the morning.

The next day, Tracy went to visit Agnes but she was having breakfast. She opened the bedroom door and was hit in the face by the same awful smell, only this time it was really strong. So strong, that she followed the smell to the wardrobe. She actually thought for a moment that something dead was inside. She opened the wardrobe doors and the smell got even stronger. She pulled away and her face grimaced. "Good god" she muttered to herself as she opened the window. She put on rubber gloves and went to fish out whatever it was making that smell.

She rummaged around in the bottom of the wardrobe and found nothing. She searched through the pockets of some of Agnes' cardigans thinking some food had been left to spoil. Then Agnes walked in. "I know what you're doing." She said as she entered. Tracy jumped out of her skin. "Oh! Agnes, you made me jump." Tracy said turning around.

"There's nothing in there making the smell Tracy. I've looked, my son has looked and now you're looking. You'll not find anything." Agnes sat on her chair. Tracy sat on the bed,

"I came to check up on you after last night. When I walked in the smell hit me, I thought…"

"Same as me love." cut in Agnes "Same as me. But there isn't anything in there. The smell comes and goes. Usually, the woman comes in but I didn't see her this morning."

Tracy kept checking in on Agnes over the next few weeks and more often than not, she would be accosted by the awful stink in the wardrobe. It got so bad that Tracy informed her manager and they replaced the piece of furniture, assuming that would rid the room the odour. Only, it didn't. The brand-new wardrobe was plagued by the same mysterious odour.

Eventually, Agnes was moved to a new room, and her old room was used for storage. Tracy later found out that the hotel was used during World War II by the army and nurses were stationed there. The clothing that Agnes had described her visitor wearing was an exact match to uniforms worn by nurses during that time period. Perhaps Agnes was seeing a nurse going about her duties?

A former employee of the care home attended my ghost walk and added some further mystery to the building. All of her experiences happened on the upper floor. A number of staff members had witnessed televisions and radios turning on and off at will, often in the dead of night. Objects being moved, doors opening and closing themselves are frequent occurrences. One member of staff had just finished cleaning an empty room in which a resident had recently passed away. She turned to leave and let out a blood curdling scream. Sat on the bed was the lady who had just died. The member of staff fled the room and refused to return.

The Turkish Baths

Built in 1897, The Turkish Baths have changed internally many times, most recently in 2018. When built, the Turkish Baths laid claim to being the most advanced hydrotherapy centre in the world. Visitors, including royalty, from across the globe, flocked to experience a plethora of water treatments which included mud baths, ice baths and steam rooms.

In March of 2022 I visited the baths in order to conduct a number of interviews with their team in regards to the apparent hauntings; I was not disappointed.

A few years previously, I had visited the baths with my wife Francesca. On that occasion I had not experienced anything paranormal, but that was set to change on today's visit.

I was early, I always am. The sun was shining but I had made the mistake of wearing a thick check shirt and coat. I stood outside of the building which lies at a busy junction on Ripon Road in the centre of Harrogate.

I entered via an unassuming side door which leads down a long corridor to the reception area. It is bright and sunny inside and the warmth clings to you like a needy child. I was greeted by a friendly receptionist and informed her of my visit. I was directed to wait on a comfy looking chair and took the time to take everything in. The atmosphere certainly doesn't evoke a feeling of dread or fear and if you were not aware of its more sinister side, you wouldn't have a clue it was haunted.

Around me were serval guests eagerly waiting to be taken through to the treatment area. In contrast to the lowkey reception, the main draw of your visiting experience is the baths themselves. Here guests are greeted by opulence, grandeur and indulgence. The stunning architecture inside has been fantastically preserved. You are taken through to the changing room area which is actually on two floors. The above area is accessed via a small flight of thin stairs and usually reserved for private treatments. Up here you will find 13 cubicles along one long wall, a small seating area and another room connected which hosts two further changing rooms, storage and sink area.

The changing rooms are Victorian in style and carved from dark wood so they stand out against the light and brightly coloured tiles. Once guests have changed you are free to explore as you wish. In the Frigidarium area, which is not as cold as its name may suggest, is a collection of sun loungers on which to relax and take in the arabesque painted ceilings and Islamic arches high above.

It was in this area in the 1960s when a guest named Susan Murton saw one of the many ghosts seen in this area. Susan, aged nineteen, was enjoying the Monday evening woman's only session. She had just finished her session in the hot rooms and was making her way back toward to the changing area when she spotted someone in a white mop cap walking through the area with the sun loungers. The figure of a girl was walking towards the pool area which is where Susan was headed, their paths would surely cross? Only they didn't, because the girl simply disappeared.

A short walk along the Italian laid terrazzo floors, you pass by the ice-cold plunge pool which fills the length of the room. This is usually enjoyed by the very brave after their hot steam room experience. The bold patterned tiles and warmth of the colours used in the glazed bricks walls are in stark contrast to the freezing waters which lie in wait for its next victim.

Rounding a corner, you cannot miss the vibrant colours of the glazed bricks as you step into the hot room zone, where three sizzling rooms wait for you. The first is the Trepodarium, or warm room, whose temperature reaches up to 120°F. Next door, and separated by a luxurious red velvet curtain, is the steam room which sits to the left of the shower area. Here, high levels of humidity combined with infused steam will cause your body and mind to relax. Next is the Calidarium, which warms you kindly at a bearable 180°F.

Beyond this is the main attraction, the magnificently hot room Lacomium, kept at a searing 210°F. Here the famous high ceilings are lined beautifully with light brown and gold tiles. A number of mahogany beds, seats and luxurious loungers hug the sides of the room. Once you have suitably warmed yourself, you can trace your steps back to the Frigidarium and if you are brave enough, you can dive into the freezing waters of the plunge pool.

Though the main purpose of the building is to provide relaxation and calm, if you work here, it can be an altogether different experience. Ghostly apparitions lurk round every corner, phantoms float along the still and quiet air and disembodied voices whisper darkly into your awaiting ear. For the stunning Islamic style arches and multicoloured brickwork seem to have retained not only the beauty of the past but also some of its former visitors.

I was here to meet and interview two members of staff, who claim to have witnessed unusual activity. The first being Louise, a friendly, knowledgeable and down to earth lady. We meet in reception where she scans the room for a more private table at which to sit and talk. There is no such table. Clearly not comfortable discussing these matters in front of guests, and rightly so, she suggested we move to the upper floor changing area which was currently empty.

I duly followed her, as it took in my surroundings with a newfound air of trepidation. Something felt different this time, I put it down to my knowledge that I was about to interview people about the hauntings in the building. I am a rational person after all. "There isn't anyone up here" Louise points me towards a small, thin staircase which, on my previous visit, I had never noticed.

I walk up the three short flights of stairs, when I reached the final flight, in front of me was a row of 13 changing cubicles. Each carved out of dark mahogany, I noted that all of the doors were kept open. My eye line swept along the length of the wall reaching the final 13th cubicle and my heart stopped.

I swear I saw something, someone in the last changing booth at the end of the row. I say nothing to my host. I am sure I saw a little old lady, with white hair and a white top, peeping out from the doorway. Turning to Louise I asked, "There's no one up here?"

Her reply was short "No. It's empty." By now we had both ascended the stairs and were in the room together. "Hmm" I mumbled as I moved towards the final cubicle and took a look inside, half expecting to see someone in there. It was empty. I took a seat directly next to it. Louise sat across from me, a small table between us. I couldn't stop looking at the cubicle next to me.

It was unusually dark considering the large windows above us. I leaned out of my seat to and looked into the 12th cubicle. Dust motes danced in the sunlight as it poured brightly into the changing booth from the windows above. I moved back in my chair and gazed into number 13. I took it in. The small space allowed little room for a single person, a small bench ran along the back of it and that was it. Simple and elegant. But there was something about it.

"I'm surprised the door was actually open." Said Louise, I turned to see she was pointing at number 13. She continued, "Traditionally, all of the doors of a vacant changing booth are kept open so you know they're empty. More often than not though, when people come up here that one is shut. We open it, only to find it closed the very next day."

"And this happens a lot?" I asked.

"All the time. I don't mind it up here. There're others that don't like it up though. Ethel, that's what we named her, is harmless enough. Every morning when I come up to clean and dust, I say 'Good morning, Ethel' and she rarely bothers me." Answers Louise.

"But she does? Bother you?" I enquire.

"Oh yes. I remember the first time I came up here. There was a sense I wasn't alone, as if I were being watched. I was so convinced there was someone up here, so I called out to them. There was no reply but I just felt unwelcome. So, every morning I tell her that I'll be as quick as possible."

"You sound like an expert at dealing with ghosts." I

retorted.

"You have to be when you work in old buildings like this."

Louise has worked at the baths for a number of years as part of the cleaning team. She loves her job and her colleagues and feels privileged to work in such a beautiful building. She's not new to hauntings though, having also spent time working at Knaresborough Museum, which is reportedly haunted.

She continued with her story. "The hot rooms are the most active for me. I was in the Lacomium, the hottest room, of course the heat was off, so it wasn't that hot. But still, it was warm enough. I was cleaning the seats when suddenly I felt cold. A cold shiver ran down my spine. But the room was warm. Then something caught my eye. Now at first, I thought it was a guest, or one of my colleagues but then it occurred to me that I was on my own that day and we'd not even opened up to the public. I was frozen in fear for a second, I didn't dare look at first. But I did. Wish I hadn't though. There at the end of the room was a shape. At first this is all it was, a form. Then it was a figure, white and transparent. It floated from one end t'other."

"Wow!" Was all I could manage. "What next?" I asked.

"Nothing. I watched it float out of sight and I went back to work. What you going to do? Run out screaming? I've work to do." She laughed.

"I tell you what was strange though. When we redecorated, the receptionist and another member of staff were in the building alone. Eloise was in reception and Mary was in the hot rooms cleaning. No one else in the building. The decorators had put up some scaffolding to get up high. Anyway, there was this almighty racket; banging metal noises, like someone was shaking the scaffolding. Now in that room, what with the high ceilings, the sound was amplified. You could hear it from one end of the building t'other. Eloise and Mary both came running to where the scaffolding was and met in the middle. They said it was still shaking as if someone had been climbing it. There was no one else there. No reason for it to be moving like that."

And with that Louise laughed and said she had to get back to work. She left me alone for a brief moment thinking about her stories. I felt as though I shouldn't be there. Like I wasn't welcome.

Then Amanda arrived. Amanda was just as nice as Louise, but I could tell by the way she held herself that she was uneasy, no not uneasy, scared.

"I don't like it up here." She announced, almost to the room, as well as to me. "Yeah, Louise was telling me about Ethel over here" I motioned my head to the door directly to my right. It almost felt as though someone was sitting in there now. I chanced a look and perhaps it was me, but the small cubicle looked darker, as though there was something, or someone, in there. I turned back to my new interviewee.

Amanda had worked at the baths for over four years.

"As soon as I started working up here, I felt uneasy. Always feels like someone is watching me. You know we keep all the cubicle doors open? Well, that one, number thirteen. The door is always shut whenever anyone comes up here. I always open it back up though, we have to. It's her doing it, Ethel. She always shuts the door. I'm surprised it wasn't shut when I came up here just now. I'm half expecting it to close at some point."

There is a pause in the conversation, "Come on Ethel, shut that cubicle door." I challenge.

"Don't say that, she'll not be happy." Amanda looks genuinely frightened.

"Ethel, if you are here, and you can hear us talking about you, close the door. Give me a sign that you're here." I demand. Nothing. In fact, I was up there for an hour and a half, and the door didn't move an inch. I even sat in the booth and tried to close the door myself. It was hard, the hinges, although in good condition, were stiff. It took some force to close the door. It certainly couldn't close of its own accord.

Amanda started talking again "She won't do it whilst we're here. I hope not anyway. The worst for me happened a few years ago. I was up here alone. No one else was at this end of the building. When I came up here, I stood at the top of the stairs and it felt odd. Like there was someone here. I put it out of my mind and went on about my usual work. Cleaning tables, the floor, dusting and polishing. And it was alright actually. The work took my mind of it. Then I moved into the next room through this archway here." Amanda turns her body to the space in the wall between the room we sit in and the next.

Next door is a smaller room, on one wall to the far left is some storage units, to its right are two changing cubicles and next to that is a sink. All built in the same dark wood as elsewhere. This room has a much less friendly feeling. It's further away from the only escape route of the slender flight of stairs and due to having less widows, it's darker. But that's not it, there is a more sinister feeling that you can't quite place.

"I was through there, cleaning and what have you. I just finished cleaning inside the final cubicle, and went into the cubicle next to it where the sink is. I emptied my bucket of water and then, BANG! An almighty loud crash shook the wall next to me. It was only the bloody door to the cubicle I'd just been in. It slammed shut with such force, I jumped out my skin and the whole room echoed and shuddered. I didn't wait around to see what the hell had done it. I moved quickly but not running towards the stairs, then I felt it behind me. A presence, so close I could feel it on my skin. Cold ran down my back, the hairs on my neck and arms shot up in fright. With more pace now, I almost ran down the stairs. But I felt it pushing behind me, trying to force me faster and faster down the stairs. I thought I might fall. I got to the bottom and, still thinking about work, I opened the cleaning cupboard to put my things away. And then it was directly behind me. Right at my back. It whispered something sinister, something unintelligible right into my ear. That scared the hell out of me. I turned round, believing there must be someone real, a colleague, behind me. I was totally alone." She stopped, almost breathlessly and took a drink of her water.

"Bloody hell. What did you do next?" I gulped, not knowing what was to come next.

"I just went back to work." She replied matter-of-factly.

"Oh. You didn't run out of there? I know I would've."

Amanda shook her head, "No, you get used to it. I had work to do." Her response was similar to that of Louise's. The team at the Turkish Baths were clearly hard workers and wouldn't let a paranormal experience get in the way of their duties.

"It seems to happen more in the mornings. I'm not even sure if anything happens when guests are in. There're a few stories but nothing that would put people off coming here, you know? But this one morning I was in the hot room cleaning, I was sat sideways on a bench and out the corner of my eye I saw this black shape. I turned to see the black form of someone floating past the shower area, across the plunge pool and out of sight. It was the oddest thing I have ever seen." Her face was awaiting a response from me.

"And you just went about your work after seeing this?"

"I certainly did. You get used to it, not that it's not scary in the moment. But once it's over you feel fine and go on as normal. There was this one time, a Friday morning, very early. I was in the Frigidarium, the place with the sun loungers." She clarified. "I was there with a colleague, the two of us talking and cleaning together when we heard this almighty splash. It had come from the plunge pool right behind us. You should've seen our faces. We looked at each other as if to say 'what the heck was that?' We got up and rushed across to the edge of the pool. The water was swelling and splashing about as if someone had just jumped into it. I looked up to the ceiling, thinking I'd see a hole in the roof where some of the masonry work had come loose and fallen into the pool. But no. There was nothing above and nothing in the water. We both stood there, staring at the water, wide eyed and horrified. Both of us unable to come up with a rational explanation as to what had just occurred. And then…"

"You went back to work?" I interrupted.

Amanda laughed "Yeah, we did."

I was facing Amanda, when her face went white and her mouth dropped open in shock. Her arm shot up and she pointed at the cubicle behind me. I turned just in time to see the door close. And just like that, the door behind me, the door to cubicle 13, which had, for the past hour and twenty-five minutes, stayed open, closed. It closed on its own. I jumped up, excited and scared in the same heartbeat. I couldn't believe what was happening. I opened the door to reveal a black chasm of a mouth staring at me. The small booth was empty. I half expected to see a figure sitting on the bench. The space inside felt uninviting. Worse than before.

"We're not welcome here" I said stepping back. I turned around to talk to Amanda about what we both just witnessed when I heard it. The distinct, high-pitched sound of a woman's voice laughed 'Ha. Ha.' I jumped, shocked at the sound which had unmistakably come from cubicle 13. It was just two syllables. 'Ha. Ha' but it sent shivers of terror down my spine.

"Did you hear that?" I asked Amanda.

"No, what?"

"A woman laughed. It came from in there." I pointed at the now open door to number 13. We both stared at the cubicle, it looked for a moment as if someone was inside, possibly a trick of the light or my mind putting something there where it isn't. Perhaps Amanda saw it too as we both stood for a while in silence. Just looking. Amanda's voice broke the stillness "Shall we go?

"Yeah." I replied quickly. We swiftly descended the stairs.

We reached the reception area and a young lady was there with the manager. Before I could relay my paranormal experience, the manager said "You should speak to Murrie here. She had an odd thing happen this other day upstairs, where you've just been." And with that she walked away, leaving myself, Murrie and Amanda together.

"What happened?" I asked. Murrie was in her early thirties and a therapist, working in the room from where we'd just escaped. "Well, I was conducting a private session with a customer and I swear a black shadow was moving around the room. Then, after the guest had left, I was sat in the room next door with all the dressing rooms. I was putting my shoes back on when I heard, from behind door 13, a woman laugh. It was high pitched and short. Almost like a fake laugh. Amanda and I shot a look at each other, eyes wide.

"What?" demanded Murrie.

I turned to her and said "Did it sound like this?" in my best high-pitched voice, I laughed, mimicking, as best I could, the voice I had just heard a few moments ago. Murrie's face dropped. "Yeah. That was it. How the hell did you know?" she probed.

"I just heard the exact same laugh a few minutes ago."

The three of us stood in silence, each of us contemplating the implications of what this could mean. I shook my head "Must have been the same voice we heard. The same ghost.

"Ethel" said Murrie. We all nodded in agreement.

I said my goodbyes and made hastily for the exit. On my way out I was stopped in my tracks by the manager. "Would you like to look downstairs? The basement area is said to be haunted as well."

I looked at my hosts and shrugged "Why not? I'd love to." I lied. I wanted to leave; I certainly didn't want to dive deeper into the bowels of the building.

Amanda led me down some stairs and through a door, marked 'staff only.' Through this private door I was struck by a deep thrumming noise coming from somewhere further into the heart of the building. "That's normal" Amanda said, as if reading my mind. "This is the staff room."

Opening the door revealed a claustrophobic feeling space. In comparison to the lofty ceiling heights in the baths, this room was comparable to a coffin, I thought. Twisting and snaking through the ceiling were a few pipes, a large table with a few mismatched chairs was tucked into one corner to my left. On the right was an office and ahead of us another door.

"I was sat in here one lunch time eating alone and I hear a knocking sound. I thought there was someone at the door behind you. I shouted for them to come in but no one did. I put my sandwich down and listened. There it was again, only this time from a different part of the room. And it came again and again, I just couldn't place what it was or where it was coming from. After four years, I'm used to all the sounds and odd noises but this was a new one to me. Never really thought much about it till I met you. Let's carry on through. I want to show you the long corridor."

She forged ahead, I followed in tow, listening to the odd noises, humming and banging of pipes. It's easy to think there are phantoms lurking beyond the walls, tapping and banging messages from beyond the veil. The noise Amanda heard could easily have just been these ancient pipes, but I don't know, after what I had just experienced, anything seemed possible down here.

Amanda took me on an unusual tour, in and out of empty and cluttered rooms. One filled with wooden relics, mahogany wall panels, mysterious wooden boxes, and long dusty benches. All of which belonged, at some time, in the building upstairs. But due to their listed status, can't be thrown away. They lounge down here in the darkness, waiting for who knows what. This room in particular feels different to the empty ones we've just visited. This room has a certain energy about it.

It is then that I am reminded of the stone tape theory. This belief came about in the 19th Century when a number of scholars tried to explain paranormal phenomena. The theory speculates that ghosts, apparitions and hauntings are the mental impressions imprinted on the fabric of buildings. This impression is usually caused by emotional or harrowing events which are then recorded onto bricks, stonework and other items. These emotive events are then replayed under certain circumstances and that is what a ghost is. You are basically seeing a moment in time replay, like a tape recording.

As I look at these forgotten pieces of the fabric of the building, it reminds me of a graveyard. The collection of objects goes beyond my sight and into the darkness beyond. Dust clings to every surface. It could do with a good clean, I think to myself.

That's it! Water.

"There is a theory" I say aloud to Amanda as we move from this room into the corridor. "About water. There is a belief that natural properties of water can intensify and strengthen spirit communication with the dead. Think about it. All of that water upstairs, and down here. Rushing through the pipes, creating energy. Spirits need energy in order to manifest, or do something like communicate, speak or move objects. So, when people visit the baths, as they always have, they come for the healing properties of the water, right?"

Amanda nods enthusiastically. "Water is calming, like a relaxing bath, or a hot steam room, it calms the body and slows us down. But equally, icy cold water, like the plunge pool, can bring about a sharp jolt of energy to your senses. This energy is actually negatively charged electrons. They become freed from the water molecules by the motion you make jumping in and causes a natural energetic reaction between body and water. So, what if, there is so much activity here because of the water itself?" Amanda, nods and smiles, I feel that she is just being polite.

"I believe in all of that. Water, energy life and death. It's all connected." Amanda stated. I think she's right.

We pass through some double doors and are accosted by the sound of a loud rumble. "That's one of the pump rooms" shouts Amanda over the din. I look into the room from which the sound is coming and see a small desk with a computer sat on it, the computer is switched on.

"People work down here?" I shout.

"Yeah, come on, through here." We exit this area through more double doors. When they closed behind us, it takes a moment for my ears to adjust.

"There's a couple of guys work down here. Making

sure the plumbing all works. This is the long corridor I was telling you about." I turn around and see a very long corridor.

"Hmm." I say thoughtfully. "It is long. What happens down here?" I turn to face Amanda.

"We use it as the staff entrance and exit. But I hate it. I always rush along as fast as I can to get out. There is a feeling that you're never alone down here." She turns to leave already. I see a few doors we've yet to explore, Amanda notices where I am looking. "Not much in them really. All full of stuff no one needs any more. Come on." She turns back the way we came, back into the noisy corridor. We exit this one and into a much quieter passageway which leads back to the staff room. And just then, the doors behind us burst open. We both jump and turn around. To our utter relief there is a heavyset man in a boiler suit moving through them.

"You gave me a heart attack!" Shouted Amanda at Karl. I was given a brief introduction to Karl. Finding out that he has worked here a long time. "Have you seen any ghosts down here?" I asked him. "Don't ask me about ghosts." He said mysteriously. "I'm not telling you anything of what I've seen." And with that he went through a door into a side room and promptly closed it behind him. I gave a look and a shrug to Amanda.

"What does that mean?" Amanda didn't have an answer.

We headed back upstairs where I thanked Amanda for her time and said my goodbyes.

As I was walking back home, I was reminded of the building's age, the sense of pride from its staff who worked in its various rooms upstairs and the all-consuming quietness that pervades from within. The stark contrast to the basement rooms below, with their mysterious boiler room man, the thrumming and banging of the ancient pipes and the ever-present feeling that you're not really alone.

The Turkish Baths are beautiful and certainly a place I would highly recommend visiting when you are next in Harrogate. Do not be put off by a few ghost stories, the luxurious pampering sessions that await you will have you forgetting all about the old lady in cubicle 13 and the numerous phantoms floating through the steam room mist.

The Odeon Cinema, Harrogate

The cinema, which sits on the corner of East Parade and Station Avenue, is one of Britain's finest modernist buildings. First built in 1936 by an architect named Weedon, it was one of the original Odeon Cinemas and has been operating for over eight decades. Internally and externally, the building has heaps of character. Its curved entrance has illuminated signage and a tall fin which thrusts from the centre, high into the air.

Inside, the building maintains many of its original features. It is here where I met with the current Cinema Experience Manager, Kevin Langford. Kevin, who has worked at the cinema for over 35 years, is passionate and knowledgeable about the building. As he explains over a coffee, "It was custom built back in 1936 with one screen. In 1971, we tripled the number of screens and a lot of building work went on. In 1989, we opened a fifth screen and in 2021, we converted the circle into two screens."

Kevin explains that much of the strange activity took place during the building work with the exception of one story. One evening, in the late 1970s, then-manager Doreen Lee was sitting in her office, organising the wage packets. She placed cash into the little brown envelopes and stored them in the safe. It was late and she was alone in the building. Doreen looked at her watch and knew her husband would be waiting downstairs for her in the foyer as usual. The front door was kept unlocked as he always let himself in.

Doreen left her office and made her way downstairs. Reaching the foyer, she was confused as to where her husband was. When she found him, loitering around outside, she beckoned him in. "What are you doing out there? Why've you not come in here like you usually do?" she asked.

"There was one of your team members waiting inside, so I just waited out here," came his reply. Doreen was perplexed.

"There's no one with me. Everyone's gone home. I'm the only one in the building." Her husband looked around the foyer and walked over to a fridge freezer full of ice creams. "He was here, like this," he said, leaning against the freezer. "Just stood here waiting. He must've wandered off at some point because when I looked again, he'd gone."

Doreen shook her head, "But I'm telling you that there's no one else on duty. What was he wearing? Maybe there is a customer in the building still." He described a gentleman wearing a flat hat, like a chauffeur would wear, a long coat with gold buttons up the front and matching gold lapels on his shoulders and trousers.

Doreen's blood ran cold. "That was a staff member

but not from this time period. Those uniforms were worn back in the 1930s. We don't wear anything like that now. Sounds like a doorman commissioners' uniform. I think you've just seen a ghost." There was another member of staff who mentioned the ghost of a gentleman, requesting people's tickets at the door, only for him to vanish when they looked down at their purses or pockets.

During construction work in 2001, a number of unusual incidents took place as work was carried out to split one screen into two. Three builders had to work through the night so that the cinema could remain open during the day. They worked into the early hours of the morning, constructing the wall. One evening, two of the workmen left to get some food, leaving one man behind. When they returned, they found their workmate had vanished. They searched the building for him but found nothing. When he finally picked up their phone call, he was in his van driving back home to Manchester. "What's going on?" asked his colleague.

"I'm not coming back. I'm off home," he snapped.

"Has something happened? Is your family, ok?" asked his concerned foreman.

"They're fine. I'm not coming back and I'm not working in that building again."

This was the only answer he gave. It was assumed that something had spooked him so much that he fled the building, leaving all of his tools behind and refusing to work there again. This strange incident happened in what is now Screen Two, about two-thirds of the way towards the rear of the building. During this work, Kevin was in the room alone chatting to his wife, Sue, on the phone. The room was still mid-way through construction work and there were no seats. The floor was made up of wood slats, a pile of which stood about five feet high at the back of the room. Propped up against this stack of wood, was a spade.

Kevin walked the length of the room, checking for fire risks while still talking to his wife on the phone. He made a mental note of the stack of plywood as a potential risk. Everything else was fine and he began to exit the room. As he turned his back to the wood pile, the spade suddenly moved sideways, clattering to the floor with an almighty crash which echoed around the huge space. Kevin, starting to feel this was unusual, quickly left the room.

A paranormal investigation team visited the building in 2012 and, while their research otherwise went without incident, they captured some compelling video footage when recording a view through the projection room porthole that overlooks Screen Two. When reviewing the footage, a team member spotted something that they hadn't noticed at the time of recording.

In the footage, a face appears on screen for a few

seconds. It was as if someone was poking their head round the corner to have a look at what was going on. There is some suggestion as to who the spirit in Screen Two could be. There has only ever been one death at the cinema. A gentleman passed away from a heart attack during a screening, sitting in the back row of Screen Two. Perhaps he is the cause of the hauntings? This does not, however, account for the abnormal happenings which take place regularly in a particular corridor behind the front of house.

The cinema had decided to introduce a new type of padlock for their fire doors. When installed, the lock prevents anyone outside from breaking in. During an emergency, you simply pull a pin, the lock disengages and then falls to the floor, allowing your escape. One of these locks was used on the fire exit for Screen One. An Odeon team member had closed this particular padlock and Kevin followed behind a short time later, checking each door was secure. Happy that the lock was engaged, he walked down the long, concrete floor to his exit.

A sudden crash reverberated in the air around Kevin. He stopped and quickly turned back to the fire exit. The padlock's pin had been pulled out, causing the heavy, metal locking system to come slamming down onto the concrete floor. This seems to happen more often than even Kevin first realised. While he was telling me that it hadn't occurred for some time, a nearby member of his team said, "Yes it has. It happened just last week!" One thing is for certain, however. The locks cannot disengage themselves so who or what is responsible remains a mystery.

During one of my ghost walks, there were around thirty of us huddled together outside of the Cinema. I decided to recount the stories you have just read when one of the group stopped me before I'd barely begun. A hand hesitantly rose into the air. "I've a story about the cinema." said a young, blonde lady. The chilling tale she went on to tell only gave credibility to what had come before.

I next met up with Katie some weeks later via a video call along with her father, Conrad Stead. I wanted to hear them both tell their story as this is the only modern ghost story in the book where two people witnessed the same thing. What makes this all the more intriguing is that neither of them had any prior knowledge of the Odeon being haunted. Not only that, Conrad was a complete sceptic. Although, after our discussion, his belief system was somewhat changed forever. Their story is as follows.

It was 2013 and the latest release from Hollywood, Gravity, was drawing in the crowds to the Odeon. Conrad and Katie loved big, exciting movies and the two of them would often go together and enjoy the latest blockbuster.

The father and daughter entered the cinema and, having purchased their tickets, were handed some 3D glasses. "These will be no good with my prescription." said Conrad, pushing his glasses up his nose.

"You will be in Screen Two," said the employee, pointing the way.

They made their way to Screen Two. Inside it was dark and the adverts were playing. It took a moment for their eyes to adjust to the darkness. Conrad pointed towards the back. "Up there," he said, struggling up the stairs. Only a few months prior, he'd had an operation on his left knee. "Let's sit here," he said, pointing at a row, close to the back. "Can I go on the end though? For my leg?" he asked.

"Yeah, fine," replied Katie. They sat. Conrad stretched his leg out into the aisle. "You'll have to move your leg if people want to get past." whispered Katie.

"Eh?" came his reply.

Katie tutted, "Your leg. You'll have to move it if people want-"

"Oh, right. Yes of course, my leg." Conrad interrupted.

The adverts finished and they both noted that no one had wanted to get past Conrad to sit behind them. He stretched out a little further and, with some relief, settled down into his seat. They put on their 3D glasses and turned to each other. Katie giggled at the sight of her dad with the oversized, plastic glasses sitting on top of his normal frames. In her words, he looked, "A right sight." Conrad jokingly wobbled his head from side to side, making Katie laugh. "Shh," Conrad hissed playfully.

The pair sat back in their seats and the film began. The opening scene was impressive and intense but spoiled by the sound of talking. Conrad heard it and, at first, assumed it was someone from the rows in front. Screen Two was fairly empty with small groups of three or four people scattered among the seats. The seats behind them remained empty. He shrugged it off and continued watching.

There it was again, only this time Katie had obviously noticed the voices too. She darted a look to her dad. There were two distinct voices which were now beginning to talk even louder. Katie tutted and ignored them, turning her attention back to the film. For Conrad however, it was different. He hated noise in the cinema. Rustling sweet wrappers and people crunching popcorn were the banes of his cinematic experience.

As Conrad listened intently, he realised that the voices were coming from behind him. But how? He didn't remember anyone asking him to move his leg to get by. He turned to face them and, in the darkness, saw two shapes sitting at the very back of the room. They were muttering away unintelligibly. "Shh!" he angrily hissed. Joining in her father's frustration, Katie had also turned around to glare as best she could from behind her 3D glasses.

The moment Conrad and Katie turned around the muttering immediately stopped. At the back of the cinema sat the two figures. Solid, grey shapes. The silhouettes of two people could be clearly seen but their facial features were invisible in the darkness. Happy that they had got the message to, "Shut up," the father and daughter turned back to the movie. It proved to be an epic film and both Conrad and Katie enjoyed the rest of the performance without further disturbance.

After the film ended, they were both eager to see who the two miscreants were. Removing their 3D glasses, the pair stood and turned to the back of the room. To their confusion, the seats were empty. Conrad looked around. "No one came past me. I would've noticed cause my leg was in the aisle."

"Over there," said Katie, pointing to the fire exit at the rear of the room. "They could've gone out that way." Conrad picked up his jacket and made for the fire exit.

"Come one. We'll go out that way. See who it was."

It wasn't that Conrad was going to accost whoever it was that spoiled the film. He was simply intrigued as to where they had gone. Conrad got to the fire exit door and pushed the lever. The film's credits were scrolling and some people had stayed around to get their money's worth. The opening door made such a loud crashing sound that everyone left in the cinema turned to see what the commotion was.

Katie looked at her dad, confused. They had left through the door and found themselves in a deserted corridor. They made their way towards a flight of stairs which would eventually lead down to the street. Conrad spoke as they walked. "If they'd gone out through that door like we did, they'd have made one hell of a racket."

"Yeah, we would've heard them," said Katie.

"Everyone would have heard them!" said Conrad as they reached the exit to the car park.

Opening the doors, they found themselves alone at the side of the building. There was no one around but them. They looked at each other, confused. "Where did they go?" asked Katie.

Her dad shrugged, "Come on." They walked back to the car in silence. Both of them going over the events in their heads.

As they drove home, they discussed what had happened that evening. It was during this conversation, they both remembered that the two grey figures at the back of the cinema were not wearing 3D glasses. Neither had thought anything of it at the time. They discussed how the two people were grey in colour, though Conrad thought that possibly the 3D glasses may have affected their vision. Katie disagreed. They both decided that the two mysterious shadowy figures were in fact grey, not wearing 3D glasses like everyone else and had left the cinema in an unknown way. Katie and her dad both agreed that the figures they had seen did not have any facial features. No eyes, nose or mouths. Nothing to say they were human.

To add to the mystery, Katie and Conrad could not decide how the unknown talkers had got to their seats at the back of the cinema. Unless, thought Conrad, they were already in Screen Two. Hiding behind the seats for whatever reason. None of it made sense to them and they discussed the matter over many dinners with their friends and family. Katie became so intrigued that she even researched any hauntings that may have taken place at the cinema. She found nothing. There was nothing to say that the Odeon was or had been haunted.

For years, it was just a story. Not necessarily a ghost story, as Conrad didn't believe in ghosts. Just an anecdote to share. It wasn't until Katie attended the Harrogate Ghost Walk that it all began to make sense to her. Katie relayed her tale to me and the rest of my fascinated guests. I was excited as her story unfolded. Neither her, her father, or in fact anyone was aware that someone had died at the Odeon in what is now Screen Two. The gentleman who had died of a heart attack at the very back of the cinema.

Could it be that this was the man they saw? Perhaps talking to a friend who was with him at his time of passing? No one can be sure what the father and daughter witnessed that night but it is incredibly interesting that neither knew anything of the history of the site. Nor did they know about the hauntings in Screen Two. So, how did two random people, with no prior knowledge, come up with a story that matches so many details from other hauntings at the cinema?

After our meeting and hearing other ghost stories about the cinema, Conrad was convinced that his encounter was paranormal. To him, there was no other explanation for it. His entire belief system has been changed and he now feels more open-minded having gone through this experience.

The Odeon Cinema is a delightful building, inside and out. You should try and catch a film in Screen Two but don't be put off if you see a grey figure, sitting at the back of the room.

The Terrifying Tale of Mr Badder

East Parade in Harrogate town centre is a lovely place to live. However, it wasn't so lovely for one particular family. Barbara and Keith Galloway lived in a small flat on East Parade in 1975. All was fine for a short time but things, as in many tales of this nature, changed quickly. It all started one day when Barbara was home alone. She was reading a book when a sudden knocking sound started from somewhere inside the flat. Barbara made her way through each room to seek out the source of the noise only to find nothing. As quickly as it began, the knocking stopped.

A moment later it started again. In fact, it wasn't so much a knocking sound, more like a door being shaken in anger. The noise got louder as though a door, somewhere in the flat, was being pounded on. She decided to go downstairs to check the flat below but there was no answer when she knocked on the door. The building was empty, save for her.

Barbara's husband worked night shifts so she frequently found herself alone in the flat. The banging noise would often return, keeping her awake at night. She frantically searched the flat and followed the sound to where she thought it was coming from. The bathroom door. She opened it quickly, thinking she would catch someone playing a nasty trick on her but when she threw the door back, there was no one there. She couldn't explain who or what was battering the door.

Shortly after this started, she fell pregnant with her daughter Lucy. Barbara didn't like the flat and certainly didn't want to bring up a child there so they applied for a council house. They were soon relocated to Newby Crescent in Jennyfields, just on the outskirts of town. They packed up all of their belongings which included: a dresser belonging to Barbara's mother, a crystal decanter given to them on their first anniversary, an old mirror they'd picked up in a charity shop and their wedding album. They set off to start their new life in their new home

They settled in quickly though times were hard for the small family. Barbara and Keith both worked hard and scraped by but they managed to raise a happy little girl in a loving family home. Lucy was around two years old when she first started to speak. She soon managed more than simple words and could string sentences together. Barbara loved to sit and listen to her daughter chattering away to herself.

One afternoon, Barbara was folding laundry as Lucy sat alone next door in her room conversing with her dolls and teddy bears. Barbara smiled to herself as Lucy was gibbering away with play talk. She noticed the tone of Lucy's voice change. She sounded agitated or frustrated with something. Barbara folded away the last of the clothes and went into Lucy's room.

The sight of Lucy, sat in the centre of her bedroom floor surrounded by her toys, caused her mum to beam at her. "Who were you chatting to Lucy?" Barbara asked as she knelt on the floor, picking up a doll and inspecting it.

"It was the man what comes to see me," replied Lucy. Barbara's head snapped up from the doll and she looked at Lucy with a frown. "What man?" she asked.

"Mr Badder," replied Lucy, matter-of-factly. Barbara felt a cold chill slide down her spine and she shuddered it away. "Lucy, you are funny." Barbara scooped Lucy up into her arms and tickled her until they were both rolling around on the floor, belly-laughing.

Barbara and Keith assumed Mr Badder was the name of Lucy's imaginary friend. Lucy had a brilliant imagination and was very eloquent so they thought she must have come up with a very clever name for this new companion. Lucy continued to have many conversations with Mr Badder over the next few months but her parents began to worry when she started having trouble sleeping at night. Lucy was suddenly frightened to go to bed. "You must go to bed or else you'll be very tired in the morning and we won't be able to go to the park." Her dad Keith was kneeling down on the living room floor, trying to persuade Lucy to go to bed. "No

Daddy, Mr Badder is in there," came her sobbing reply.

"I'll go in there and get him out." Keith made a show of going into her room and dragging My Badder out by his ear. Lucy stifled her giggles as she clung to her mum, the pair of them watching as dad made a drama out of it. "There you go, and you can stay out there all-night Mr Badder!" said Keith as he mimed throwing someone out into the hall. He took Lucy in his arms and the family went into her room. "There you go," said her mum. "Dad's thrown him out. You can go to bed now."

Lucy did go to bed but she would not sleep. She would lay awake, night after night, in utter terror. She grew paler and paler and her parents started to worry when Lucy began refusing her food. Barbara and Keith were sat at the dining table one tea time, trying to bribe Lucy to eat something. Lucy just stared vacantly ahead refusing. "What does this Mr Badder look like, Lucy?" asked her mum, hoping to bring Lucy out of her stare. Lucy blinked at her mum.

"He is tall with hair on his chin. He has a long dark coat with nice buttons on it and on his sleeves too. He has a tall hat on his head which is flat on the top. It's black. I don't like him anymore."

Barbara and Keith didn't know what to do. Worried about her health, they took Lucy to the doctors. Keith was hesitant to tell the whole truth but Barbara thought it was best to be honest about their situation. So, they told the doctor everything in the hope that he would give Lucy something to help her sleep. The doctor listened intently to their story, making notes here and there and nodding his head. When they had finished, he placed his pen down and folded his arms, smiling at Lucy who had sat still and quiet the whole time. Rather unusual for a toddler, the doctor had thought. Usually they get bored, start crying or wander around the room looking for some sort of entertainment. "It is highly unlikely for a child of Lucy's young age to have developed such a detailed imaginary friend, let alone for her to hold such long conversations with them," he said. "I'm going to suggest something a little out of the ordinary. The situation you are in, I feel, calls for it. I recommend a visit to the local spiritualist church for help. I am sure what you need is spiritual guidance to be rid of this, Mr Badder." They were both lost for words at what the doctor had prescribed. They decided not to take up his advice and went home, hoping Lucy would eventually grow out of it.

One evening, in the height of summer, it was sticky, hot and humid. Lucy was playing in her room at the back of the house where it was a little cooler. Barbara was downstairs washing up. Small beads of sweat were forming on her brow. Suddenly, she heard a loud scream coming from upstairs. Barbara leapt into the hall, taking the stairs two at a time and ran into Lucy's room. When

Barbara opened the door, she was hit with an icy blast of cold air. She moved through the wall of freezing air to where Lucy was curled up in a ball crying. Through her sobs, Lucy said, "He was here, Mummy. Mr Badder was in here. I don't like him. Get him to leave."

Barbara and Keith let Lucy sleep in their room from then on, though Lucy didn't get much sleep even then. Her parents were at a loss as to what to do. Then, one day, Keith suggested something. "I think we should call David."

"David Fox?" asked Barbara.

"Yes. You know people think he has psychic abilities. He might be able to help." David was an old family friend; he was Keith's best mate and a window cleaner by trade. David had always been different. He told others he'd had a number of paranormal experiences himself and had the ability to see and feel spiritual energy. David would often help people out who needed it. He seemed to have an incredible gift though he never used it for financial gain or notoriety and kept it between close friends. He would often give guidance from visions he said he'd had of the future.

In their minds, David was a very good, trustworthy man and Lucy's parents had no reason to doubt him and all the reasons to trust him. Barbara called David the next day. The phone rang as Barbara was rehearsing in her head what to say when he picked up. "I know what you're ringing for. Lucy has a visitor, doesn't she?" Barbara dropped the receiver in shock. Picking it back up, she said, "How the Hell did you know that? How did you know who was calling?"

David simply replied, "I'll pop round tomorrow if that's alright? What's your new address? I'll have to stay over a few nights to see what's happening." David took note of their address and readied himself for a battle.

The next day, David arrived. He asked Keith and Barbara not to tell him anything of what had happened. He wanted to use his own skills to assess the situation and not be influenced by any information. The first night, David, Keith and Barbara were downstairs talking when they heard Lucy scream from her room. David rushed upstairs, opening Lucy's bedroom door. He was taken aback by what he saw. Standing by Lucy's bed was a tall man in Victorian clothing and a black top hat, leering over the little girl. The man turned and quickly disappeared.

Barbara and Keith entered the room just in time to see the figure vanish. They now shared their daughter's terror. They didn't know what they were going to do. "I'll just ask him to leave," said David later that night as the three of them sat sharing a bottle of wine. Lucy slept quietly on the sofa.

"Do you think that'll work?" asked Keith.

"Dunno to be honest. He feels like a much stronger presence than anything I've felt before, so, I'm now not sure that it will do much good," said David.

"Worth a try though," pitched in Barbara.

With Lucy fast asleep on the sofa, the three adults stood in the kitchen. Holding hands in unity, David asked the spirit to leave the family's home. He recited a few words and they broke the circle. Things only got worse.

Days later, Barbara was ironing in the living room when Lucy said to her, "What's he doing here, Mummy?"

Knowing they were alone in the house, Barbara tensed and replied, "Who? There's no one there!"

Lucy smiled at her mother and said, "Yes there is. He's right behind you." Barbara froze with fear. She tentatively turned around slowly with glassy eyes. "What's he doing?" asked Barbara.

"He's going huuhuuhuuhuu," said Lucy in a menacing tone, making heavy breathing noises. Barbara rushed over to her daughter, bundled her up in her arms and ran to the neighbour's house.

Weeks went by. Anna, their neighbour, was asked to babysit one evening while Barbara and Keith went to the local working men's club for a drink. When they arrived home, a couple of hours later, they were shocked to find Anna in tears saying that she was never going to babysit again, refusing to tell them why. Though they never found out the reason, they believe to this day it had everything to do with Mr Badder.

Feeling desperate, both parents realised it was time to make a call to the spiritualist church. They explained the entire story from its beginning in East Parade. They were told that they had a malevolent spirit in the house and the only way to get rid of it would be for a specialist priest to perform an exorcism. This news was something that Barbara and Keith would have baulked at previously but it now felt like a ray of hope. They arranged for someone to come out and visit them the very next week.

The family began to hope that things might get better. As Lucy was becoming increasingly withdrawn and sleep-deprived, her parents decided they would try anything to get their happy little girl back to normal. It wasn't a conventional method of seeking help but, to them, it wasn't a conventional situation. Unfortunately, the day before the priest was due to arrive, they received a telephone call from the spiritualist church to say that the only qualified priest in the district that could perform exorcisms had sadly passed away. There was nobody that could come and help them. Not for a long while anyway. They were alone.

Once again left without help or hope and feeling like there was little else they could do, Keith decided to redecorate Lucy's bedroom in an attempt to brighten it a little and lift her spirits. As he pulled out the wardrobe to paint the wall, he noticed the old mirror that had been wedged down the side of it. It had come with them when they moved from the old flat on East Parade. The mirror was originally from the inside of an old Victorian wardrobe. It wasn't much to look at, had no frame and was of little value so he decided to take it to the tip.

He bundled it into the back of the car, drove it down Wetherby Road and threw it into the skip. He was quite surprised by the sturdiness of the thing as it crashed against the iron side of the skip, remaining fully intact as it landed. He drove away thinking nothing more of it. After that day, Mr Badder never made another appearance. Not once. Not for Lucy, at least.

The Nightmare House

Aged eleven, Leslea Petty lived in a fine house on King's Road. Her father worked for the Commonwealth Graves Commission, mending and replacing gravestones. Often, he would bring his work home with him. Their garden was a tapestry of broken headstones. The garden path featured a number of discarded sections of gravestones and an ornamental rockery displayed a number of tombstone pieces. Little Leslea was home alone one afternoon. Sitting in the living room, reading a book, she was struck by something along the back of her neck. Leaping to her feet and screaming in fright and pain, she turned around. There was just a wall behind her. Thinking something may have fallen, such as a picture frame, she looked around on the floor, finding nothing. Another evening when in bed, she lay awake, reading. She stopped mid-sentence when she felt someone shift their weight, sitting on the end of her bed. Frozen in fear, with her view obscured by the book she was reading, she felt something slowly creep along the edge of the bed towards her. Her heart beat faster and faster, fear welling up inside her. Just as the movement reached her side, it was gone.

As an adult, Leslea suffered from the occasional nightmare. These haunting dreams always took place in her childhood home or at the flat she lived in between 1998 and 2001 in the centre of Harrogate. In her forties, she moved into a flat on Raglan Street in the centre of town along with her young daughter Francesca and their cat Axl. The tall building was attached directly to a spiritualist church next door. The Harrogate Spiritual Healing Church was established in 1943 under the leadership of Miss Flint. The church is still in use today and they are very proud of both their heritage and their stunning building.

As well as being next door to the church, Leslea's flat sat above the Harrogate Liberal Club, a members-only snooker club where she worked full time. She loved her new home and its simple layout. It had a modest bedroom, living room and bathroom with stairs leading to the street. Her bedroom had one unusual feature. A fire exit. This exit led directly into the spiritualist church. All was fine for a few weeks until, one night, she awoke for no apparent reason. Then she heard it. Music. Piano music. She listened; her ears attuning to the sound. It was coming from the church next door. The volume of the music rose and became so loud it kept her awake most of the night.

The next morning, tired and angry, she decided to complain and headed to the church. A lovely lady answered the door and Leslea explained what had happened. The lady looked puzzled and said, "I'm sorry but the church would have been locked at that time of night. No one was in here. If they had been they couldn't have been playing a piano. We don't have a piano in the building." Confused, Leslea went back to her flat, questioning what she thought she had heard.

It was night time and Leslea woke up, again, for no apparent reason. Her eyes were drawn to the fire door at the foot of her bed. She saw something move in the strip of light, visible at the base of the door. Whatever it was, it was working its way through the gap. A black shape emerged into the room. It was the biggest spider she had ever seen. It stood there for a short time and then scurried back from whence it came. This happened on a number of occasions. Leslea began to think that this arachnid could have been the physical form of the spirit which was haunting her flat and place of work. Then, one night in bed, Leslea turned over to see the spider had actually come right into her room. It began running towards her bed. She jolted upright and looked at it in horror. The spider stopped, turned around and ran back beneath the door. She eventually lay back, thinking about this incredibly unusual behaviour for a spider.

The next time Leslea awoke, at around 3 A.M, she listened, expecting to hear something abnormal. She heard a sound she recognised. In the snooker hall, several retractable chords hung from the ceiling with chalk at the ends allowing players to reach up, dust their cue tips and with a crack, release them back. The familiar whir of the chords echoed from below. She shot out of bed and put on her dressing gown. She thought someone had somehow gotten into the snooker hall and was having a game. Quickly checking her daughter was fast asleep, she went downstairs to the main snooker hall, the room where the sound had come from. Flicking on the light switch, she could see the room was empty. Looking up to the ceiling, she was taken aback to see a number of the chalks which were suspended by chord were swaying back and forth. There was no apparent reason for this, no draught, no one around. She locked the door behind her and made her way back to her flat. An almighty racket sounded behind her followed by the smashing of glass. She rushed back towards the room she had just left.

She nervously opened the door and turned on the light again. She was shocked to find a picture of a former club president had fallen from the wall. The photograph was oddly propped up against the wall below where it previously hung. She looked closer only to find that the nail on which the picture had been hung was still in the wall. The string which hung on the nail had not snapped. How had it fallen, she thought? The glass in the frame had smashed but the broken pieces had been piled up neatly in front of the photograph, not scattered about as she would have thought they'd have been from the fall.

On another occasion, Leslea was alone in the same room and she felt a cold finger poke her in the arm. She turned, assuming someone had come into the room without her noticing, but she was alone. As she turned to leave, out of the corner of her eye, she spotted a black shadow moving across the room.

The door to her flat had a large, heavy security bolt high up on the inside. Leslea judiciously kept this bolted at all times, fearful her young daughter would leave the flat and fall down the stairs. It was always bolted. One night, Leslea was awake in bed when she heard the deadbolt slowly moving with its familiar scratching, sliding sound. Terrified that her daughter had somehow managed to climb onto something and reach the lock, she shot out of bed. In the hallway, she turned on the light to find the front door ajar. She rushed to her daughter's room to find her fast asleep in bed. Leslea closed and locked the door before searching the flat for an intruder. She found no one. Leslea moved out not long after and shudders every time she thinks about her flat on Raglan Street.

The Harrogate Club

Victoria Avenue is my favourite street in Harrogate with its double-width road built for horse-drawn carriages, large leafy green trees and stunning Victorian buildings. It is home to Harrogate's best-kept secret. The Harrogate Club. The double fronted, Victorian property has played host to the private club since 1886. The club itself was formed on 13th July 1857 by a group of local businessmen and men of independent means. They created a public reading and news room, first located in the lounge of Gascoigne's Hotel. Here, members could meet to read a selection of journals and newspapers.

In 1886, the club moved to Victoria Avenue where it remains today as a private club, though they now welcome female members. The building is impressive both inside and out with high ceilings and huge windows. Every room has been refurbished to recreate the Victorian splendour of yesteryear. The building is like a time capsule. Members can still enjoy lectures, dinners, fine dining, bridge and snooker.

The club has always been a place for opulent enjoyment and relaxation. Its former members include Samson Fox, industrialist and philanthropist (great grandfather to actors Laurence and Amelia Fox). Sir Titus Salt, who built Salts Mill and the UNESCO World

Heritage Site, Saltaire Village, was a regular and the architect of Leeds Corn Exchange, Cuthbert Brodick was a visiting member. They were followed by Baron Ferdinand de Rothschild who was also a member and it is rumoured that J.R.R. Tolkien frequented the club at some point.

The author and creator of Sherlock Holmes; Sir Arthur Conan Doyle was a regular visitor to The Club at 36 Victoria Avenue. He loved Harrogate and would often visit all year round. In 1920, it is rumoured that he invited his best friend to the club, the world-renowned escape artist and magician; Harry Houdini. It was in this very club where a séance was held with Doyle and Houdini (allegedly) in attendance.

Doyle and Houdini's friendship was an unusual one. They became friends when Houdini sent Doyle his latest book, Arthur then invited Harry to visit him at his home in Sussex. Houdini had planned a UK tour so the pair met on 14th April 1920. They came to Harrogate the same year and, after the séance at the club, the pair went to seek out the Cottingley fairies near Bradford. The fairies turned out to be hoax photographs taken by Elsie Wright Frances Griffiths. Doyle was so convinced that the photographs were real that he used the images to illustrate an article he wrote for the Christmas 1920 edition of The Strand Magazine.

The Harrogate Club itself is said to be haunted by

a number of ghosts from its distinguished past. One evening in 1999, a cleaner was finishing her duties upstairs when she stopped in her tracks. Frozen by fear, she had the feeling that someone was behind her. She slowly turned to face the room and found it to be empty. Still, she stood transfixed by a feeling she couldn't explain. Then she heard, as clear as day, a man uttering the words, "Will that be all sir?" She fled downstairs and phoned her manager, who quickly returned to the building to help conduct a search, only to find they were the only people in the building. The cleaner believes she heard the voice of a servant, speaking to a club member from days gone by.

Another member of staff claimed to have been leaving the building one night and, as she turned behind her to retrieve her coat from the coat stand, was shocked to see a handsome and well-dressed gentleman standing at the foot of the stairs. He wore a black, tailcoat suit, black shoes, a cape and tall top hat. The lady blinked and the apparition disappeared.

Downstairs, where the club's offices are located, you may find the ghost of a former staff member who wanders the lower ground floors at all hours of the day. This particular ghost enters and exits rooms at will, almost as if they are not aware that they are no longer living. The Harrogate Club is still in use today and I would urge you to visit. At the time of writing, there are heritage open days in September where the general public can book to visit. You could even become a member and enjoy all the club has to offer, including its ghostly guests.

The Old Courthouse

The Courthouse in Harrogate sits on Raglan Street and was the town's first police station, built in 1866. Harrogate became a borough in 1884 and subsequently a court was introduced. It was home, until recently, to a family law firm and, as of 2022, the building is due to be turned into flats. The new owners are likely to be unaware that the building is never vacant. Beneath the building are the basement and former cells where they kept those who were arrested. It is in the bowels of buildings where unusual activity takes place.

In 1996, a young man by the name of Matthew Bee was on his work experience placement at the law firm. Matt had enjoyed his first few days working in the offices. Everyone was friendly and he was treated like an adult. He was tasked with going down to the basement to retrieve some files. As he made his way downstairs, he was inexplicably overcome with fear. He didn't want to look silly in front of anyone so he made his way to the bottom of the stairs with his heart racing.

He took a few breaths and tried to control himself. It wasn't like the basement was scary. It was a little dark and dank but nothing seemed unusual about it. Even so, Matt couldn't shake the feeling of dread creeping over him. He looked around to orientate himself. There were smaller rooms off the main corridor and it was inside one of these that he went looking for the file in question. He scanned the shelving unit, trying to locate the file. He stopped. The room felt charged with electricity and the hairs on his neck and arms stood up. Then, without warning, the files began flying from the shelves. It was like something from a horror movie. Paper flew everywhere as Matt ran from the basement, up the stairs, out of the door and all the way home. He would later get into trouble with his school for the mess he'd caused and even more so when he refused to go back to his placement.

Grove House

Situated on Skipton Road is the Grade II listed building, Grove House. On this site was the former inn, the World's End, which is believed to date back as early as 1728. Over time, the building has been an inn, school, home, orphanage and a care home for the elderly.

It has a very interesting and mysterious past. Inventor Samson Fox (actors Amelia and Jamie Fox's great-grandfather) once lived here. It is rumoured that Samson built a secret underground laboratory where he conducted his experiments, the entrance to which has never been found. Samson was a true local hero. He built Grove Road School which is opposite his former home. He also funded affordable social housing for locals as well as providing money to build The Royal Hall.

His inventions helped to put Harrogate on the map. He built the water gas plant which provided the town's main street with some of the earliest street lighting in the country. He is the only person to ever be Mayor of Harrogate for three consecutive years.

The building was bought by Mrs Holland and transformed into a boarding school in 1805. In 1927, the building was used as a children's home, ran by the Royal Antediluvian Order of Buffaloes (RAOB).

You can still find their motif embolised on the railings around the building.

During the Second World War, part of the children's home was used to accommodate British and American service personnel. The building retains a wealth of period features such as wooden panelling throughout, ornately carved archways and a huge stone-carved fireplace, held up by two naked mermen. In 1998, renovation work uncovered ornate plaster panels above the music room. Thought to be from the days the building was The Dragon Hotel, they were carefully removed and valued in excess of £40,000.

The building has stood empty for a number of years. Though some may be unsure why, locally it is known that there have been a number of reported hauntings from different time periods.

When the building was being used as a care home, residents would often be heard laughing and giggling when alone in their rooms. When staff enquired about the source of amusement, residents replied, "It's the children. They've come to play again." There were never children present in the building. Perhaps, as one former staff member surmised, they were the orphans from the children's home?

A number of people have reported seeing servicemen in uniform, walking the grounds and its empty corridors. One morning local postman Max walked down the long drive to the front door. The gravel crunched beneath his feet and his breath held in the icy cold air. He posted the mail and turned to admire the gardens when he spotted something out of the ordinary. A man wearing a soldier's uniform was standing in the centre of a large patch of grass. "Morning." Said the Max. There was no reply. The figure of the soldier walked away into the bushes. Max, thinking this was strange walked across the grass. His footprints were left behind in the morning dew. He reached the area where the figure had been stood. Looking down Max noticed that the grass was void of any other footprints save for his own. Where had the man gone? He was nowhere to be seen.

The most unsettling and exciting story is said to happen every Christmas Eve. It is rumoured locally that on Christmas Eve, the large metal gates of Grove House fly open as if pushed by an unseen force. Then, from out of the darkness, a horse-drawn carriage rumbles down Skipton Road rushing at speed into the grounds of Grove House before promptly vanishing into thin air.

I've yet to leave the warmth of my house on a Christmas Eve to try and witness the phantom carriage for myself, but who knows, one day I just might.

Hoopers Department Store

Hoopers Department Store first opened its doors in Torquay in 1982. Its Harrogate branch dominates the high street with its four-storey building and huge signage at the front. The store was managed for years by Mr Hewlett. He was a friendly man who loved the store and was a very good employer by all accounts. He liked a cigar and was often seen smoking inside the store. He sadly passed away in the shop on its main staircase, in front of the building's clock, which hung high on the wall. That day, the clock stopped working at the exact time he died.

Thirty-year-old Jane Wharton worked in the store during the 1960s. She was working alone on the top floor where its offices were located. She took a break to use the bathroom and, as she walked along the corridor back to her office, she stopped. She could smell smoke but not from a fire. It was the unmistakable smell of cigar smoke. She recognised it as her old manager, Mr Hewlett, would smoke the same brand in this very corridor. It was then she noticed a light haze, like dust passing through sunlight. She thought back to when he was alive and, with a shudder, carried on back to her desk.

Jane didn't tell anyone about her experience and thought it was best to keep it to herself. A few months later, she was working alone in the lingerie department on the corner of the second floor. It was a Wednesday and it was unusually quiet. She had only had three customers all day. This gave her ample time to organise and sort through some of the clothing on display. She had her back to the shop floor as she sorted through some bras. "Hello, can you help me?" a customer asked. Jane turned around with a smile and found herself alone. "Hello? Madame?" Jane called out. She walked around her counter and onto the main shop floor. Looking around, she found no one nearby. She momentarily left the room to see if she had heard someone at the door. Again, there was no one to be seen. Searching the fitting room, she was convinced now that she was alone. She had definitely heard someone but couldn't find the source of the voice.

Jane later told some of her colleagues about both experiences. She said it was like opening a floodgate. Suddenly, everyone was sharing stories about the smell of cigar smoke and disembodied voices. She wasn't alone in her experience and found comfort in that.

The Westminster Shopping Arcade

At 32 Parliament Street sits the iconic Victorian Shopping Arcade which is the last of its kind in town. It was originally named The Royal Arcade when it first welcomed customers in 1898. It is home to a collection of independent shops, a tearoom, a health food shop, an art gallery, a hair salon and Harrogate's only supply shop for witches. The architecture, inside and out, is wonderfully Victorian. The inside has the look and feel of Diagon Alley, the famous street from Harry Potter. The collection of quirky shops, signs, stairs and balconies add to the atmosphere of your shopping experience.

It is thought that the arcade stands on the site of a house formerly owned by a witch, known then in the 16th century as a cunning woman. She would have acted as an early form of midwife and delivered babies for the local woman who could not afford a trained doctor's service. The house is thought to have sat exactly where the current health food shop is though we will come back here later. Come the 1800s, it was then home to Dr Titus Deville M.D.

Doctor Titus was a force to be reckoned with in Harrogate. He was a rather vocal man, especially against the council and their lack of public hygiene. The good doctor railed against the system and was outspoken about the absence of a good sewage system in town. How could Harrogate claim to be at the centre of health and spa treatments when there was excrement and urine freely flowing down Parliament Street, the street on which he lived? There was a problem with the town's sewage system and the council were slow to spend money on it.

Titus was so vocal about his concerns that he spoke out publicly against the Harrogate Improvement Commissioners. The commissioners tried to silence Titus and took him to court, hoping to remove him from his position at the Medical Office of Health. The commission was unsuccessful and, at York Assizes where serious crimes were dealt with, Titus counter-sued the commission and won.

Inside the arcade is a curious little shop where you will find the very welcoming Joanne Mayben. Jo has worked in The Cauldron of Curiosity since November 2021 and went on to take ownership in 2022. This atmospheric merchant of the metaphysical, new-age artefacts and magick, is Harrogate's only witchcraft supply shop. My favourite part of this delightful shop is the dedicated Psychic Parlour, a secretive and mysterious room where private readings take place; it really feels akin to the Victorian parlour rooms of the 1800s. If you ever visit Harrogate, then take a trip to this brilliantly independent shop and stop by for a private reading, it really is a hidden gem.

The shop was once located in Unit 8 which is now a bridal shop. It was here where the activity began. It started with a cupboard door which would open on its own accord, never when anyone was around, and only at night when the shop and arcade were closed. Each morning, Jo would open the shop to find the usually stiff doors that had opened at some point during the night.

The only other unusual occurrences were the dodgy electrics. Every single morning, when you first turned on the lights, it would trip the electricity in the shop. It would only trip once and was fine for the rest of the day and it did not happen in any other unit. However, Jo did not put this down to the paranormal, instead blaming old wiring or perhaps a power surge.

A year passed and the doors continued their evening ritual until Jo moved the shop to the smaller adjoining Unit 10 where it remains today (as of 2022). It was here that the activity ramped up a gear. Whatever spirit or spirits haunt the shop, they have an affinity with cats. Speaking with Jo, she began, "Anything to do with cats, such as cat images or ornaments, will be moved during the night. One day I came into the shop and there were two cat ornaments sat in the middle of the shop floor. I had left the shop that night and they were Sellotaped to the shelves where they were on display. I came in the next morning and they were six or seven feet away from their shelf. Just sat there. Upright." There was no explanation that Jo could think of that explained what she had witnessed. "There was also a picture of a cat and that kept moving around the shop too. It would be on a shelf. I would leave for the night and return in the morning to find it in the middle of the floor." As Jo was telling me her story, I noticed that all of the activity she described took place at one particular end of the shop. This just so happens to be right next to the wall of Unit 8 where the cupboard was located which would open of its own volition.

Every Thursday, the shop opens late and it was during these hours that Jo witnessed something that she can only describe as other-worldly. She was sitting in her shop, busying herself with some odd jobs, when she felt compelled to look out of the window. Outside she could see the closed tearoom opposite, closed for the night. She looked back to her work when she performed a double take and looked back to the area outside. Her eyes were drawn to a small flight of stairs which lead up to a hair salon. Coming down the steps was a black mass. It had no legs but looked as though it was trying to take the form or shape of a human. It floated across the floor, right past her shop to another set of steps where it vanished. Jo has seen this mysterious black mass at 8:30 P.M on four separate occasions so far.

Who knows, perhaps this paranormal event takes place every night at the same time and Jo has only witnessed it on the nights she happens to be working late?

Jo and I are well-known to each other. She hosts alternative events at her shop and I am one of the regular performers alongside Jo, who has her own incredible abilities. One of the events I was witness to was a paranormal investigation led by Chris Myers of North Yorkshire Paranormal Investigators. Chris is a very knowledgeable man. He uses everything from dowsing rods and Ouija boards to mirror scrying in his investigations. He is always quick to debunk anything and does not claim that everything is paranormal. I like this about Chris and Jo. Two people who are passionate about the supernatural world but are always the first to think logically about anything that they, or others, experience.

One of the teams on the investigation was in the basement conducting a Ouija board session when, without warning, the board flew across the room. I was witness to a group communicating with the spirit of a child who seemed to know an awful lot about the mother of one of the guests in our group. They were using a spirit voice detector, a device which scans a collection of words and plays them at random. A lady asked, "Who is with us?" and it just so happens the random collection of words picked out were MUM,

YOURS and KATH. The woman asking the question had a mum named Kathleen who had passed away. It could have been a coincidence but, in the surroundings of this haunted arcade, even I was unsure what to make of it. Jo hosts alternative events throughout the year and I would encourage anyone to book a ticket to experience this truly special place in Harrogate.

Downstairs in the Arcade, you will find Quality Health Foods which has provided our town with a wide range of healthy, natural and organic products, supplements, herbal remedies and body care lines for over thirty-five years. Its owner, Linda Le Floch, is a qualified biochemist and nutritionist and her shop stands on the spot where the former cunning woman and Doctor Titus once lived.

One day, Linda was alone in her shop when she noticed something in her peripheral vision. Though she had not seen anyone enter the shop, there appeared a young lady. Linda looked at the girl. She was wearing old-fashioned clothing and a housecoat in pinks and purples. On another occasion, Linda and another shop owner saw the same apparition from outside of the shop. The girl was standing in the same location as before. One interesting account, which mirrors the activity taking place in The Cauldron of Curiosity, is that of items being moved. Many times, Linda or one of her team had entered the shop, only to find that random items had been removed from the shelves and placed in the centre of the floor.

If you want a shopping experience with a difference, Westminster Shopping Arcade is the place to go. With its collection of fine, independent shops and spooky happenings, you are sure to have a great time exploring this peculiar arcade.

Harrogate Theatre

At the centre of town is our Grade II listed theatre. The Harrogate Grand Opera House, as it was once known, was designed by Frank Tugwell, the same architect who designed The Savoy Theatre in London and the Futurist Theatre in Scarborough. In 1900, the doors were opened for the first time with a charity show for soldiers fighting in the Boer War. The theatre still retains many original features, fixtures and fittings as well as an actor who refuses to take her final bow.

Everyone knows that all theatres have their own ghost, and Harrogate Theatre is haunted by the spirit known locally as Alice. There are no mentions of her in the theatres archives but it is believed that she was, at one point, an actress working at the theatre. The most common story attributed to her is that she was the lover of the theatre's director with who she was secretly having an affair. As she begged him to leave his wife, he fed her empty promises. Alice turned to alcohol which soon led to an addiction. She would take a drop of peppermint oil on her tongue in order to hide the smell of her affliction. The relationship turned sour and one drunken evening, after a bitter row with her lover, Alice jumped from the top balcony into the seats below where she died.

Her appearance and hauntings usually start with the sudden smell of peppermint in the air. The temperature will suddenly drop and you feel the overwhelming sensation that you are not alone. There are numerous stories about Alice moving objects. She has been known to steal props and put them in odd places. One actor tells a story of a pocket watch which vanished from their props table, only to turn up in their dressing room later on.

Alice is often blamed for stealing the seamstresses' scissors, moving costumes, and generally causing havoc backstage. It seems that she is blamed for any poltergeist activity at the theatre.

In 1990, an usherette was alone on the top balcony, cleaning the seats. The noise of her vacuum cleaner filled the vast space with a thunderous sound. She turned it off for a moments rest and peace. It was then that she realised, she wasn't alone. An icy, cold chill threaded through her spine when her eyes met with a whitish-grey apparition, manifesting in front of her.

It was in 2000 when an electrician was working alone on the stage. Suddenly his nostrils picked up the strong smell of peppermint. Confused, he stopped his work and stood up on the stage. Looking out into the audience, he called out and received no answer. He turned to go back to his job when he saw an orb of light floating in from the darkness on the right-hand side of the theatre. It elongated into a pillar of light, exactly at the spot where Alice is thought to have jumped from. The brilliant blue light then shot across the auditorium and disappeared into the darkness. Being an electrician for a number of years, he had no explanation of what he had just witnessed. By all accounts, Alice is a friendly ghost. The staff are rather fond of her and, troublesome though she is, mainly think of her as harmless.

Ashville College

A shville College was the first school funded by the United Methodist Free Church. In 1875, the Church Assembly decided to establish a college that promoted sound and advanced education. The independent school, which was built in 1877, has many secrets including military bunkers and a few hauntings too.

During World War I, around three hundred of the boys at the school were called up to serve, thirty-eight of whom lost their lives including eight who died in the Battle of the Somme. When the Second World War broke out, the college was requestioned by the RAF and the boys schooled there were evacuated to the Lake District. Four hundred and sixty-eight pupils volunteered for the armed forces with a loss of fifty-nine lives and decorations being awarded to ninety, Old Ashvillians.

A number of bunkers used during the war remain hidden beneath the grounds and, along with them, the apparitions of several former RAF soldiers have been seen walking the corridors of the old school.

The most famous haunting is that of The Green Lady who is said to appear in the clock tower and corridors around the college. The ghost of a former sister who worked in the school's sanatorium, she has been witnessed by pupils and teachers alike many times over the years. There were even reports of the spooky nurse haunting the school as far back as the First World War. It is believed locally that the woman's lover died and so she threw herself from the clock tower though my research cannot find such a death reported anywhere.

Haverah Park, Harrogate

Three miles west of Harrogate is the small parish of Haverah Park. With a population of around thirty people, it is a collection of widely dispersed farms accessed by private roads or footpaths.

Over 200 years ago on 18th July 1812, the newspaper, the Leeds Mercury, printed a story which caused a stir. One Sunday evening between seven and eight o'clock, two local farmers named Anthony Jackson and Martin Turner were inspecting their cattle on Havarah Park, near Ripley. Martin was suddenly surprised to see an army of phantom soldiers in white military uniforms. The soldiers were marching over the brow of a hill and in the centre was their commander wearing a scarlet tunic.

The two men could not believe their eyes as several hundred men marched towards their position. The two farmers hid beneath some heather only 100 yards away and watched in utter disbelief as another larger group of soldiers, dressed in dark-coloured clothes, appeared marching behind the white army. The huge army then vanished beneath a mysterious thick cloud, obscuring the spot from which the men disappeared. The two farmers stood up and searched around only to find no trace of the enormous army.

Glebe Avenue

No. 24 Glebe Avenue is a four-storey town house, just off Cold Bath Road. It was occupied by Rosemary Enright who lived there ain the 1980s as a divorcee bringing up her only child, a daughter who was at boarding school during term time. This fact may be relevant, at least to the first incident.

Immediately following a half-term break teenage daughter, Charlotte, had gone back to school after a week's holiday. Rosemary went up to her room on the third, or attic floor of the house to clean. Her bedroom also came with a small sitting room. They were untidier than even she usually left them and Rosemary was somewhat furious to find plates of half-eaten food under the bed. However, she kept her temper under control and just got on with the extensive tidying and cleaning job. She heard an unusual sound which was redolent of a large map or poster falling off a wall. Going out of the sitting room to see what have might have made the noise she saw at once that the large poster depicting some whales had fallen off the wall behind Charlotte's dressing table. She thought little of it.

When Rosemary had finished cleaning the sitting room, she moved onto the bedroom and bent down to fish the whale poster out from behind the dressing table where it had obviously fallen to the floor. But it was not there and it could not be found. Rosemary searched the immediate area. It had not slipped underneath the close fitted carpet; how could it? Nor had it skidded between the skirting board and the wall; there was no gap, nor had it somehow fallen sideways to lodge behind the nearby linen press. Might it have somehow slipped under the carpet? Rosemary couldn't take it up to look at that point. She left the poster to its fate, confident that her daughter would likely not notice. Several years later when Rosemary sold the house, she had the removal men untack the carpet and look for the poster. They found nothing. To this day, they have no idea where the poster went.

There were several small incidents of this kind during the time the two ladies lived there, especially when Charlotte was at home. The poltergeist never took anything of value or importance, just something that it was a nuisance to lose. Doubtless this phenomenon was due to the psychic energy projected by adolescents, particularly girls.

A more dramatic incident took place one November night which Rosemary felt was impossible to explain and very frightening. She had returned home late after a meeting of the Bradford Textile Society, where she was the editor of the BTS's magazine. She rushed upstairs to her own sitting room to turn on the television. There was

a programme about the paranormal on at 10:00 P.M and
a number of distinguished "television scientists" were
to set up and participate in a variety of experiments.
Rosemary was very interested in the paranormal and
this new show was bound to be exciting.

Whilst watching intently, she became aware of an
unusual amount of noise in the house adjoining hers;
a late Victorian terrace which was divided into 3 flats.
There seemed to be a great deal of thumping and
running up and down the staircase. The sound insulation
of the houses was poor but this was a far greater
level of noise than she had ever been accustomed to
hearing before. She continued watching the television
programme whilst feeling vaguely uneasy. The noise of
hurrying footsteps continued next door. At one moment
Rosemary suddenly felt nervous that the front door was
not locked and bolted as it normally was. She had run
into the house in a rush. Had she forgotten to lock up
when she came home? She couldn't sit there without
checking. She went out of the sitting room where the
television was, walked along the short landing until
she stood at the head of the stairs and could look down
the hallway. No, the door was locked and the recently
fitted, large brass bolts shot home into their housings.
Reassured, she went back to her programme. Rosemary
listened as the presenter asked members of the audience
at home to go and find a spoon to put on top of their

televisions so that Uri Geller's metal bending efforts might affect our own spoons at a distance. Keen to join in, she went down to the kitchen to fetch a cheap metal spoon. Placing it on top of the television she continued watching the programme until another uneasy feeling swept over her.

There was some sort of sound on the floor below and a gust of cold air wrapped itself around her, whipping up some loose papers on the coffee table. She quickly shot up from the sofa and rushed back to the head of the stairs. The front door now stood wide open and the cold night air was pouring into the house. The brass bolts had their tongues shot forward, projecting beyond the edge of the door as if in the closed position but they were free of their housings which were completely intact and undamaged. It was an awful moment in all senses. Bizarre and utterly frightening.

Reluctantly, she crept downstairs, closed and locked the front door, and shot the bolts home. It was all she could do. She couldn't call the police, there was no intruder. She reluctantly checked every room. Rosemary went to bed that night with all the lights left on and did not sleep. In fact, she kept the lights on all night and for many nights afterwards.

Perhaps that the fact Rosemary was watching a television programme about the paranormal at the time of the incident is irrelevant. Perhaps it is not. It could be that the two things were inextricably linked. Was the extraordinary behaviour of the front door connected to the house itself? I rather doubt it. Was it connected to her personally, possibly. Or was it in fact the result of psychic energy generated far away in a London television studio? Who knows for sure?

Tales From Beyond

Surrounding Harrogate are some of the prettiest towns and villages you are likely to visit in Yorkshire. From Knaresborough, Birstwith Village to Spofforth and Ripley they all lure tourists in with their cobbled streets and chocolate-box facades. But lurking inside the quaint cottages, castles and country pubs are a whole host of sinister stories.

The classic English village of Ripley has the most picturesque castle, a famous ice cream parlour, an ancient church, a country pub and plenty of ghostly tales to tell. The castle is home to the Ingilby family who have lived there for over seven hundred years. The original village was torn down in the 19th Century by one of the Ingilbys. The castle and church are all that remain of the old village. The family rebuilt it, modelling it on the Alsatian Village in eastern France.

Ripley Castle, Harrogate

The Grade I listed, 700-year-old castle was originally a 14th Century house. It is surrounded by a deer park; a Grade I listed gatehouse and Grade II listed gardens

And ornate bridges, which straddle Ripley Beck. The stately home has been the seat of the Ingilby baronets for centuries, starting with Sir Thomas in 1290 who acquired the castle through his marriage to Edeline Thwenge as part of her dowry.

Sir William Ingilby had ownership of the castle in the 1500s and two of his sons were impassioned Catholics on the run from the authorities. His son Francis, a priest, was caught hiding in a priest hole at the castle. He was taken to York where he was hung, drawn and quartered for not renouncing his faith. His screams can still be heard in the tower where he hid.

It is the ghost of Dame Alicia Ingilby and her children however who are a constant source of mischief at the home of the present Lord and Lady Ingilby. Lady Emma Ingilby has reported that, when her son was a baby, she would often feed him in bed. Tiredness would overcome her and she would briefly fall asleep, however she would be woken up by someone tugging at the bedclothes or shoving her shoulder. There was of course no one in the room but she always felt that someone was keeping a helpful watch over her and her baby.

Dame Alicia Ingilby lived in the castle during the 1800s. She sadly lost both of her two children; Henry aged five and Mary aged three, to Leukaemia in the 19th Century. It was this tragic event that triggered the poltergeist activity which still haunts the family home to this day.

The first reports of any paranormal activity were in the mid 20th Century when a fireplace was discovered during some renovations in the Tower Room. The discovery of the fireplace, hidden behind wood panelling, let loose a poltergeist. After the fireplace was discovered, the room was locked and the workmen left for the night. Their return the next morning brought utter shock and confusion. Opening the door, they discovered that furniture had been knocked over, paintings had been turned to face the other way and even the face of a great grandfather clock and been removed. The family are used to the poltergeist activity and one story hit the newspaper headlines in 2017 when four Georgian candlesticks reappeared, three years after vanishing. On Christmas Eve in 2014, Ripley Castle was decorated with an abundance of seasonal decorations. Closed for the season, the Ingilby family were enjoying some family time. Lord Ingilby went to the strong room to retrieve the set of four candlesticks which they traditionally displayed on such occasions.

The candlesticks were missing and though a thorough search was conducted, they were not found to be anywhere in the castle. Sir Thomas proclaimed with utter confidence that the poltergeist had taken them and would return them in due course. So convinced was Sir Thomas of this fact, he would not report the items as being stolen. His family tried to convince him to refer the matter to the police but he was adamant that they would be returned. Many searches of the strong room and the castle took place during this time but the candlesticks were nowhere to be found. It wasn't until two years later in May 2016 that Sir Thomas finally relented and reported them as stolen. Weeks later, the insurance company paid out £8,500 to purchase replacements. In the summer of 2017, the replacements had been bought and the family went to place them in the strong room for safety. There, sitting on a shelf, was a bright red, Christmas-themed carrier bag. The bag had not previously been there, even though the room had been searched a number of times. The red bag clearly stood out in the room. The replacement candlesticks had been returned and the money was given back to the insurers. The story was so astonishing that it made national headlines.

The ghost of Alicia has been seen by many guests and staff members over the centuries. She is a benevolent spirit, meaning no harm and is believed to be responsible for a lot of the activity at the home. She has been seen many times; wearing a flowing dress and walking down the hallway towards her children's old nursery where she then floats straight through the closed door. It is Alicia who is often blamed for the disappearance of small items such as scissors, cutlery, watches and keys. These items will vanish completely and then will simply turn up in a random place, months or even years later. A silver dessert spoon from a cutlery set vanished from its display box for 18 months. It then inexplicably reappeared back in its rightful place, inside the locked wooden canteen storage unit.

A young man, who joined me on the Harrogate Ghost Walk, told me that he was friends with the current Ingilby son. "We grew up together and I would stay over there a lot," he began. "I would sleep in the guest room which I believe was the nursery belonging to the two children who died there. Often, in fact on many an occasion, I would wake up and see Alicia sitting on the end of my bed. She wasn't scary. Not at all. She felt calming and kind-natured."

It seems that Dame Alicia is seen by many people. One tourist was being given a guided tour when, out of nowhere, what he assumed was a costumed actor walked right past him wearing a long flowing dress. "She looked terribly sad, almost as if she had been crying. I assumed she was playing the part of one of the family members but when I looked again, she had vanished. No one else had seen her and the guide suggested that I had just met Dame Alicia Ingilby. I'd never seen a ghost before and have never seen anything since so this really sticks in my mind."

Her children, Henry and Mary, are also held accountable for some of the more mischievous hauntings. A former member of staff explained, "Personally, I've had keys go missing. It's not like I've left them lying around. They're attached to a lanyard which is hooked to my belt but I'll be walking around and suddenly notice that the keys aren't jangling about. When I look down, the keys are gone. I used to retrace my steps, thinking they had dropped off. Now I don't bother. I know that they will turn up later on, usually somewhere random. Some people have noticed that the ghosts of the children are more active when there are babies or other young children in the building. I know Lady Emma had some experiences with her little one. Guests at weddings have also complained to us of unusual things like cutlery moving on tables and their children sometimes complain of being followed by an invisible friend."

In 1997, a woman and her husband visited the castle for a private tour with a guide. When the lady, who was pregnant, entered the banqueting hall, she felt uneasy.

Almost as if she were being watched. As the tour guide was talking about the history of the room, the lady looked around to take in the various features being pointed out. It was then she noticed a white smoke or mist, emanating from one of the other visitors. Her first thought was that he was smoking but no one else had noticed the strange white cloud. A few moments passed and the guide had finished their historical speech. He asked if anybody had heard that the room was haunted. The guide pointed to the exact spot where the strange smoke had appeared and proclaimed, "That is where the ghost is always seen." By then, the smoke had gone completely.

The castle is used for many events, parties and weddings. A guest at one wedding in 1992 left the party to use the bathroom. After washing her hands, she went to leave the room, only to find the door handle wouldn't budge. She tried it multiple times but it was as if someone was holding the handle on the other side. She knelt down on the cold floor and looked at the gap between the door and its frame. The door wasn't locked and the latch bolt was not engaged. She looked through the old key hole and thought she saw movement on the other side. She shouted, "Hello? If this is a joke, it is not funny. Open this door now." She began to get across as she was missing the festivities and she had travelled a long way for the wedding. She began hammering on the door, trying the door handle continuously and shouting at the top of her voice.

After ten minutes she was fighting with the handle, which just wouldn't budge, when the door suddenly flew inwards, nearly knocking her off her feet. She was furious. "Are you ok madam?" asked a concerned member of staff.

"I've been trapped in here for about 15 minutes. Someone was holding onto the door handle. Was it you?" She demanded answers.

"It most definitely wasn't. I came past and heard you shouting and opened the door and there you were. There was nobody out there at all," said the confused staff member.

"Well, someone locked it then because I've been trying the handle this whole time and it wouldn't open." The guest left the toilets and was stood in the corridor.

"I'm afraid the door doesn't lock. We don't even have a key for this one. It was lost." Just then a couple of the children from the wedding party ran down the hallway laughing and playing. The staff member pointed at them. "Perhaps that explains it. I hope you are ok. Can I help any further?" she asked.

"No. That's fine. Probably was the kids." But the guest was not wholly convinced. She even spoke to the children and their parents, only to find that they had been with them in the main room the whole time.

Ripley Castle has played an important role throughout history. In 1603, King James I was a guest at the castle but, come 1605, nine of the eleven known conspirators of the Gunpowder Plot were either relatives or associates of the family. The group even stayed at the castle during the plot itself. The family were Royalists and in support of Charles I during the Civil War, they took arms against Oliver Cromwell. One famous family member stood at the front line. She was nicknamed Trooper Jane. Jane was the sister of Sir William Ingilby but a law, brought in by King Charles I, forbade women to fight in the war.

Jane was not about to sit idly by while her brothers went off to fight. She donned full body armour and rode into battle next to her brother, William, at the Battle of Marston Moor, the largest battle fought on English soil. However, the Royalists were defeated, losing four thousand soldiers during the two-hour-long battle.

Jane and William survived the slaughter and fled back to their family home. Here they changed from their battle armour and dressed for bed. It was not a moment too soon. Oliver Cromwell, who they were earlier battling to the death, turned up at Ripley Castle. He was looking for somewhere for him and his troops to rest for the night. William, fearing for his life, hid in a priest hole whilst Jane answered the door, armed with a pistol in each hand! She pretended to be alone and terrified, refusing the army entry to the castle. Due to her cunning, she convinced Cromwell to force his men to sleep in the barns and not the castle itself. She knew that, if they were let inside, they would search the property, likely finding and killing her brother.

Cromwell himself was allowed to sleep in the castle. Jane gave him a chair downstairs to rest in and demanded he stay there and not leave the room for the sake of her honour. Jane, as brave as she was, held a vigil outside his door. Sitting in a chair, pistol in each hand, she waited until morning came. Jane undoubtedly saved her and her brother's lives with her quick thinking, good acting and absolute bravery.

At first light, Cromwell and his troops left for London but they had a number of Royalist prisoners in tow. Cromwell lined them up against the castle wall where they were shot by firing squad. On the ancient battlements, you can see a number of bullet holes from the musket fire. These tell-tale signs are a stark reminder of the castle's history. The ghosts of these soldiers are said to still haunt the walls today. Many people have seen ghostly apparitions of civil war soldiers marching up and down the wall in the dead of night.

The castle is open much of the year and is a wonderful place to visit.

The Boars Head, Ripley

Karen Perkins is an internationally best-selling author, selling over one hundred thousand copies of her award-winning Yorkshire Ghost Stories: *Parliament of Rooks, Knight of Betrayal, The Haunting of Thores-Cross, Cursed* and *Jennet*. I love Karen's work and implore you to seek out her books.

Karen and I spoke for an hour via video call. She grew up in Harrogate and, many years ago, worked at the Boar's Head in Ripley before a career in banking and financial services. She was a competitive sailor, gaining the ladies title in the European championships, and has now found her calling as an independently-published writer.

It was her experience at the Boar's Head which shaped her professional writing. As a child, Karen, who grew up in Birstwith Village, had a number of imaginary friends. She often knew things that she shouldn't or couldn't have known. Back in the early 90s, The Star, as it was formerly known when it was a coaching inn, underwent a huge refurbishment and became The Boar's Head. The then-twenty-year-old Karen started working there soon after the hotel had opened its doors.

Karen worked on the reception and loved her job. It was December and Christmas was fast approaching.

The season had been a quiet one. Being a new hotel, it took some time to become established so Karen often found herself with little to do. Not one to shirk her responsibilities, she always found something to fill her time. One evening, in the quiet and empty hotel, Karen was alone. Christmas decorations hung from the walls and the obligatory seasonal music played on repeat. From her position at the reception desk, she had a clear view of all the exits as well as the annex, a small row of rooms where the former coachman had lived, along with the stables and storage rooms, now a collection of luxurious ensuite rooms.

Karen was bored. No guests were booked in so, feeling on edge, she decided to check the rooms and stock up on the stationery and other items which may be needed by guests. She finished the main hotel during the evening and then made her way to the annex. Stepping outside, there was a chill in the air as she walked the path towards the annex. She worked her way through each room until she reached Keepers Cottage. The double-height building consisted of the former stables downstairs and above would have been the groomsman's accommodation. Karen methodically worked through the two downstairs rooms and made her way to the final three above.

She walked into Room 3 and felt sick. The room made her feel nauseous but she wasn't sure why. She thought to herself, what an awful room! She stopped to take it all in. The room was actually lovely; decorated by a renowned Harrogate interior designer. It was a stunning room and one she should feel at home in. But something wasn't right.

Feeling uneasy, she quickly saw to the task at hand and left the room. Turning to lock the door, Karen was struck with frozen terror and could not move a muscle. An ice-cold chill ran up her back. She was stuck, albeit only for a few seconds, and could not move. Something passed through the door, through Karen and into the corridor behind her. In that moment, she was released from her frozen spell.

Behind her came the chilling sound of a childish giggle. The girl's laugh was made all the eerier by an accompanying swishing sound; almost as if the girl were running her hands down the walls as she ran away from the scene. Karen waited no longer and bolted for the exit. Flying down the stairs at full pelt, arms outstretched, she burst through the outside door. Luckily for her, she had not closed the heavy door properly or else she may have broken her arms after hitting it at such a speed.

She kept running and found herself back at the hotel's reception. She ran into the kitchen and found the chef. Explaining her story, the chef was dismissive and didn't believe her. Karen was shaken so she left the hotel and crossed the short distance to the housekeeper's cottage where her colleague, Barbara lived. She hammered on the door and, as Barbara opened it, the older lady looked at Karen with surprise in her eyes. "Good lord Karen, you look like you've seen a ghost," she said, ushering her friend inside. Cup of tea in hand, Karen relayed her paranormal experience to Barbara. Barbara assumed it was all in her imagination. Working alone in one of the most haunted villages in Yorkshire and barely out of her teens, Karen must surely have imagined it.

"Come back to the hotel and we can look around. I'll show you there's no ghost," the housekeeper said, as she escorted the terrified Karen back to the scene of her haunting. They picked up the chef on their way to the annex. He too was convinced that Karen had imagined it all. The three of them checked out Room 3 first. Everything was as it should be and even Karen had to admit that the room felt normal.

They moved down the corridor in the direction the ghost had seemingly ran. They looked inside Room 4 where everything was also normal. When they approached Room 5, Karen looked at her companions with a frown on her face. It sounded as though there was someone inside. A voice could be clearly heard. Barbara unlocked the door and the three of them were hit with an icy chill. They looked at each other in utter confusion and disbelief. The furniture in the room had been moved. It wasn't as if the room was untidy but pieces of furniture had been purposefully and oddly repositioned.

Barbara was most taken aback as she had been in this room only an hour or two earlier to do her final checks before finishing her shift. She knew the furniture had been in its rightful place. Now, the room stood in disarray. The television was the source of the voices they heard. It had been turned on and, oddly, was now facing the wall. The dressing table stool was in-between the twin beds, and the window was open when before it had been shut. The chef simply stood momentarily in silence before eventually walking away in disbelief.

Later as they sat in the reception, Karen reminded Barbara that many guests who had stayed in that room had often complained of the TV changing channels by itself, as well as the windows opening and closing. Karen had also noticed that activity was reported in the room when there was only one person staying there. Nothing ever happened if two guests or more were staying in the annex wing.

The annex is not the only part of the hotel which is haunted. During the renovations, a workman was busying himself in one of the drawing rooms in the main part of the hotel. He stopped in his tracks when he saw a woman in old-fashioned clothing walk straight through a solid stone wall. The point in the wall where the woman had passed through was later revealed to have once been a door.

During the same period of time, a plumber was working alone upstairs when he too saw a lady wearing a long dress and a bustle walk straight through a solid wall. He was so frightened by the experience that he ran screaming from the building, leaving his tools behind and never returning to reclaim them. Unusually, the ghost of the lady hasn't been seen after the renovation work was completed. Perhaps her spirit was disturbed by the ongoing work?

Elsewhere In Ripley

Just outside The Boar's Head is a cobbled square and it is here that, during snowfall, two young children have been seen having a snowball fight. They appear for a while, having fun, and then simply vanish. It is thought that they could possibly be the children of Lady Alicia Ingilby.

Across the road is Orchard Lane. One evening, a local man, who knew the area well, drove down the lane to visit friends. He turned left at the corner and standing in the road was a young couple. Swerving to avoid hitting them, he crashed his car into a wall with a thump. Exiting the car, he surveyed the damage. There was a dent and a few scratches. He turned to confront the young couple only to find they had disappeared. He assumed they had done a runner. However, his friends later told him that he wasn't the first person to crash their car in the lane. Two other people had swerved to avoid a young couple standing in the road, only for them to vanish into thin air.

Marston Moor

Six miles west of the city of York, tucked between Long Marston and Tockwith, is the site of one of the biggest and bloodiest battles in English history. Visiting today, you will find billowing cornfields lining the road from Long Marston to Hessey. Thanks to its dark past, this quiet and idyllic setting has its fair share of ghost stories.

The 2nd July, 1644 saw the Parliamentarians and the Royalists take part in a grizzly battle on Marston Moor. The Royalists, led by Prince Rupert, were trying to liberate the Marquess of Newcastle who was being held in York. The violent battle saw around four thousand Royalist soldiers die while three hundred Parliamentarians lost their lives.

The infamous site of this great battle is haunted by a number of ghouls. Ghostly sightings have been reported here as far back as 1886, when historian, William Camidge, told of local stories mentioning soldiers stained with blood, wandering the neighbourhood while a headless officer astride a phantom horse rode wildly in search of the battle. Yet these stories are said to be folklore. The real stories are told from personal accounts.

In November 1932, two friends were driving across Marston Moor on a cold night. The driver slowed the car as the pair witnessed, twenty yards ahead of them, three men wearing purple-coloured robes and unusually large hats, tilted to one side, walking along a ditch by the road. They drove past them and slowed but the men had vanished. When they told their story, the duo was shown a drawing of Cavaliers from the Civil War. The men announced that this is exactly what the three figures looked like.

Again in 1968, the sighting of around half a dozen men dressed in 17th Century attire were seen by a party of tourists as they drove along one of the country roads of Marston Moor. The tourists slowed down beside the men and, as they looked drunk, drove on believing they had just seen a group of actors taking part in some sort of battle re-enactment. No re-enactment, of course, had occurred. Later, when they told their story in a local pub, they found out they had actually been driving along a road where the actual battle had taken place.

In 2016, in a field just outside of Marston, a local farmer had reported unusual activity. In the searing summer sun, he had just finished ploughing a field and decided to cool off by the river. He left his tractor and took a short walk down to the riverside. He removed his shoes and socks and paddled in the shallows. Taking a seat on the dried grassy bank, he lay back and closed his eyes. A few moments into his well-deserved rest, he heard the unmistakable sound of chattering. A number of men were talking. He assumed a large walking party had gotten lost. Sitting up, he looked around to find he was alone. The voices carried on mumbling to each other. Unintelligible conversations were taking place all around him, along with the odd sound of clinking metal, like armour or swords, he thought. They were joined by the sounds of horses cantering past and stopping somewhere behind him. He turned, expecting to see some local riders but he was shocked to see only his tractor in the distance. The sounds were all around him now and so he stood up, socks and shoes in hand and ran back to his tractor. On his way there, he noticed that the sounds had stopped. He found out later that it was on this exact spot where Oliver Cromwell had camped his troops, shortly before the battle of Marston Moor.

Spofforth Castle

Five miles south of Harrogate is the pretty little village of Spofforth. Best known for the 13th Century castle ruins, the village gains its name from a combination of spa and ford, likely due to its location near the River Crimple. It is first mentioned in the Domesday Book of 1086 when William de Percy lived in a grand manor house on the site. It is thought that the terms of the Magna Carta were drawn up at the castle in 1215 and then later presented to King John.

Spofforth Castle is on a small rocky outcrop overlooking the picturesque and peaceful village. All that remains of the former medieval manor house is part of the principal apartments from the west part of the property. A steep flight of steps leads down to the site of a former courtyard. To the right are a couple of large rooms. There is a spooky passageway which was cut into the rock but is now blocked. There are the remains of a row of columns and low walls around the site, an under croft and a private chamber that can be reached via a door in the northwest corner. A tower holds a spiral staircase which takes you up to the first floor. The castle would have been rather spectacular to behold but is now nothing more than a haunted ruin.

In the 11th Century, the site was home to William de Percy who built a manor house here, it is believed to be the location where rebels drew up the Magna Carta in 1215. The remains you can see today are those of a fortified manor house from the 14th and 15th Centuries.

The Percy family supported the House of Lancaster during the War of the Roses and as such, the castle was attacked in 1461 by the Earl of Warwick and his army who burned the castle to the ground. It wasn't until 1559 that Lord Henry Percy, restored the building. The castle was reduced to its final state during the Civil War when, in 1924, the Baron of Leconfield transferred ownership to the state. It was left to rot and ruin.

One recorded sighting is that of a woman seen jumping to her death from the tallest tower of the castle. The bluish-white apparition is always seen in the same spot, standing in the small parapet at the top of the tower. Here, she hovers for a few moments before jumping to the ground below. What makes this horrifying manifestation even more hideous is that the woman is only half a person. Her lower half is never seen beyond her jumping to the ground. Nobody knows who she is or what her story was but she was spotted in 1973 when two tourists were enjoying a picnic at the site and prior to that a whole group of schoolchildren and their teacher witnessed the haunting in 1969.

Fountains Abbey

Britain's largest monastic ruin lies hidden behind six hundred and fifty acres of stunning woodland, parks, lakes and ornamental gardens. Now in the ownership of the National Trust, it is a site my family and I often visit, so I know it, and its spooky stories very well.

Along with the ruins of the abbey is a fine Jacobean manor house named Fountains Hall. Built by Sir Stephen Proctor, who bought Fountains Abbey estate in 1597, the home was constructed between 1598 and 1604 using stones taken from the abbey ruins. The most famous of its ghosts is that of Sir Stephen's daughter, known as The Blue Ghost. She has been seen wandering her former home, day and night by both staff and visitors alike.

The main hall has a couple of ghosts, including a man who materialises through the wooden panelling, as if walking through what may have once been a door. He is dressed in Elizabethan clothes and is completely unaware of any living person in the room at the time of his appearance. When the hall is locked and the front doors shut, an unusual occurrence often takes place. One day, when the ruins were open to the public but the Hall was closed for maintenance work, a tourist named Sue Marley and her husband Alan approached the main doors to have a closer look at the woodwork. It was here that they heard the unmistakable sound of a group of musicians, rehearsing a sing-along. They couldn't place the musical style, nor had they heard the song before, but the rehearsal went on and on. The group went over and over the same part of a song as if trying to perfect it.

A member of the National Trust team approached the curious couple and informed them that the hall was unfortunately closed. Sue replied, "Its ok, we knew that. We were just listening to the rehearsal." The staff member looked confused and began unlocking the door. "Rehearsal? Inside the hall?"

"Yes, there's a band playing and a girl singing," replied Alan. The staff member unlocked the door and stepped inside to find an empty room. This has happened many times.

In the hallway leading from the main hall, visitors have been walking away when footsteps quickly approach them, running loudly towards the hall. They were passed by an invisible entity rushing by. On the old stone staircase, the voices of two children can be often heard playing and laughing. It is on these stairs that a phantom rainfall can be heard pattering against the windows, even when it is a hot, dry summer day.

Upstairs, in one of the grand bedrooms, visitors have been woken in the night to the sight of a shadowy man carrying a candle, with a dog by his side. Upon approach, they both simply vanish. In the very same room, children have witnessed a spectral lady dubbed the Shining Golden Lady. This enigmatic phantom only appears to children who are sick or unwell. She sits with the child and strokes their hair, offering kindness and comfort. If the children speak to an adult about the lady, she evaporates before their eyes.

Outside, in the ruins of the Abbey, there are yet more spirits. One of which is supposedly the abbot, William Thirsk. Thirsk was executed by King Henry for plotting against him. His ghost has been seen walking the grounds during the day. Inside the Chapel of Nine Altars, which still stands, visitors have experienced the disembodied sounds of Benedictine chanting. There are even reports of a choir singing hymns. The beautiful, yet incredibly eerie sound, echoes around the ruined site.

Knaresborough

Three miles east of Harrogate is Knaresborough, a picture postcard village with a labyrinth of medieval streets and steep, stone staircases which weave their way up and down the hillside. On top of the hill is a 12th Century, Norman castle which lies in ruins. Here, the castle boasts the most stunning views across the River Nidd to the magnificent railway viaduct which straddles Nidd Gorge. The river provides the many tourists who flock there with boats to hire as well as a crossing point for the famous Bed Race. The Knaresborough Lions Club hosts an annual Bed Race on the second Saturday in June. Established in 1966, the race is a fancy dress pageant which includes a gruelling 2.4-mile time trial course, ending with a swim through the icy River Nidd. All the while, a team pushes a bed through the town with a driver atop. I'm not making this up. It is a spectacle to behold and you should see it at least once in your lifetime.

There are a number of curious stories which come from Knaresborough. There is The House in the Rock named Fort Montague. In the 19th Century, an odd child was born into the Hill family, who lived in the house. The child had incredibly blonde, woolly hair, like that of a sheep. I'm not sure why but he became known as the Woolly-Headed Boy of Fort Montague.

Then there is the rather unusual, Chapel of Our Lady of the Crag. This Grade I listed shrine on Abbey Road is dedicated to the Virgin Mary. Built by John the Mason in 1408 when his son, who was presumed dead in a rockfall in a local quarry, was found alive.

The town is also home to the oldest chemist shop in England which first opened its doors in 1720. There is a story that one morning, a chemist entered the shop and found that one of the cupboards was open with its contents laid out on the counter. Afraid there had been a burglary, she went to the police station not far from the shop. Upon inspection, it was found that the cupboard had not been tampered with, it had been unlocked. Yet, the chemist had the only key. Further still, nothing had been stolen though items from the dispensary cupboard had been removed and placed in neat little groups on the counter top. It remains a mystery as to what went on in the shop. It could well have been paranormal as Knaresborough has its fair share of ghosts.

Mother Shipton, Knaresborough

Home to the infamous cave and the petrifying well, I can't talk about Knaresborough without mentioning Mother Shipton. Though not a ghost at all, Ursula Sontheil, was born in 1488 to a young lady aged fifteen, called Agatha Soothtale. The mother and daughter were outcasts from society and forced to live in the cave. Eventually, the mother was rehomed in Nottingham and Ursula was placed with a foster family in Knaresborough. Mother and daughter would never see each other again.

As Ursula grew up, she displayed unusual gifts. The local population came to respect her talents as a herbalist and people would visit her for healing remedies. Eventually, she met and married Toby Shipton, a local carpenter. She took his name and became known as Mother Shipton. They lived happily for a number of years in Toby's home. Tragically, Toby died young and Ursula was blamed for his death by the townsfolk. Shunned once again and grieving the loss of her beloved husband, she moved back into the woods and the cave from where she was born.

Mother Shipton's fame spread far and wide and she became a household name with people travelling from across the country to seek out her potions and spells. She claimed that she could see into the future and made a number of prophecies about the people in Knaresborough. Some of these came true and soon word reached the king. King Henry VIII contacted the Duke of Norfolk and wrote of a Witch of York. This is believed to be a reference to Mother Shipton.

Her prophecies included, "Water shall come over Ouse Bridge, and a windmill shall be set upon a Tower, and a Elm Tree shall lie at every man's door." This left the locals baffled as to its meaning. That was until the town gained its own water source. This was achieved by creating pipes made of elm trees which carried the water over the Ouse Bridge to a windmill which drew the water through the pipes and into every man's door in town. Ursula died in 1561 but you can still visit the petrifying caves where she was born.

Knaresborough Castle and Grounds

A bove the river, perched high on a rocky outcrop, is Knaresborough Castle. It was built by the Normans around 1100 to keep those living in the North quiet. By 1066, the Normans had all but conquered the entire country but the Northerners rebelled and fought back. William I, known as William the Conqueror, squashed the rebels and burned everything to the ground. Crops, homes and farms were destroyed while animals and people were slaughtered north of Trent. After this event, which became known as the Harrying of the North, the king built a number of castles in order to remind everyone who was in charge. It became the ruin you see today during the Civil War when it was a Royalist stronghold. Cromwell ordered the destruction of all Royalist castles in 1648 and Knaresborough Castle was destroyed. Much of the stonework can be seen dotted around town as it was repurposed to improve people's homes.

The castle also plays a key role in a famous historical murder. The slaying of Thomas Becket took place on 29th December 1170 at Canterbury Cathedral. Becket was an advisor to King Henry II but the pair did not see eye to eye. One day, after a furious row, the King is said to have shouted, "Who will rid me of this troublesome priest?" Four of the king's knights took this as an order and set about a plan to rid the King of Becket.

They went to Canterbury and entered the cathedral unarmed. They demanded that Becket come with them to Winchester Court to answer for his actions against the King. Becket had no intention of doing such a thing and joined the monks so the knights left. The incident was seemingly over, however, the knights had simply left to arm themselves. Upon seeing this, the monks barred the doors but Becket is said to have told them to open the doors as no one should be locked out of the house of God.

The knights attacked Becket, laying blow after blow to his head with their swords. The first blow cut off the crown of his head. The second hit his head but Becket stood firm. The third blow brought him to his knees. The fourth and final blow took the top off his head, spilling blood and brain matter across the Cathedral floor, staining it red. The knights fled to Knaresborough Castle, the home of one of the attackers, Sir Hugh de Morville. Here the three men waited for a year for things to blow over. During this time, it is said that the men were wracked with guilt and remorse. It is no surprise then that a ghostly manifestation has been photographed in the castle which may depict the gruesome murder of Thomas Becket.

In 2000, a curious photograph was taken inside the castle itself. In the image, you can see two male figures.

One of them is laying on the floor with an arm raised, as though defending themselves. The other figure has their arms raised in the air, as if striking the man on the floor. Could this ghostly, white mist show the murder of Becket? Perhaps Sir Hugh de Morville was so wracked with guilt that his memory of the event has been imprinted on the castle stone and plays out like an ethereal scene from a movie.

One day, a woman was walking the grounds of the castle. Enjoying the views, she failed to notice that she was now walking behind someone. After a moment, she looked forwards and saw a lady dressed in white. It was only when she looked down to the ground, she saw the lady in white had no feet. This caused her to freeze to the spot and, just at that moment, the footless lady turned around and faced the walker. To her utter horror, the ghost turned around and, where her face should have been, was blank. There was a complete absence of features.

On another occasion, a tour guide was hosting one of the town's infamous Knaresborough Knightmares ghost walks, usually led by local man, Mark Ellison, when he stopped to tell a story and they saw a ghost. The guide was talking to a group on the castle green when they noticed an extra person had joined the tour, a lady. When they looked more closely, they noticed the woman, who was dressed all in white had no feet. More so, she seemed to be void of a face. It is thought that she may well be the maid of Queen Phillipa who was wife to King Edward III but another tale says that she is the wife of the castle's jailor. No one knows why she has no feet or face but she is one of the town's more terrifying ghosts to witness.

The Courthouse Museum

Knaresborough Courthouse Museum sits in the grounds of the castle. It is well worth a visit. It is believed to have been built by Sir Henry Slingsby of Scriven, 1st Baronet. He was, at one time, the constable and surveyor of the castle and once a powerful man. He mainly dealt with minor offences such as financial disputes and tenancy agreements. Other more serious crimes included cutting tree branches to feed livestock in the winter months and gathering acorns and apples. How very dare you! On top of these heinous crimes, he had to deal with poaching and people milking other people's cows. Yes, milk theft.

The two-storey building is made of limestone and brick. Internally, it still retains many stunning features, including a 14th-century fireplace and 17th-century doors. The beautifully-restored courtroom proudly displays 16th-century benches and wooden panelling.

The building has its very own ghost too, believed to be that of the beheaded Sir Henry Slingsby. Sir Henry was a Royalist and was executed for his part in a conspiracy to restore Charles II to the throne. He was initially taken to Hull, where he was jailed for a short time, before being relocated to York. A second plot was uncovered and the government made an example out of him. He was tried and found guilty of treason in London, in March 1658. He was executed on Tower Hill on the 8th of June of the same year.

Above the entrance hangs his portrait. Also displayed is his bloodied white shirt, which is believed to have been what he wore at the time of his execution. Every morning, one of the staff members named Jean unlocks the doors and enters beneath the portrait and every morning she says, "Good morning, Sir Henry." Jean is simply being polite as she owes Sir Henry a debt. At the end of a long day of tours and work, Jean was leaning against a display case, texting her husband to come and pick her up. She sent the text and then suddenly dropped her phone. It hit the top of the case and fell down the back. "Oh no," she cried out loud. Jean reached behind the case but couldn't reach her phone. Her colleague, an elderly lady, came to help. "Perhaps we can move it?" she suggested. The case was large, made of oak and as solid as a rock. "Let's try," said Jean. The pair lifted, heaved and hefted but the case didn't move an inch. "It's no good," breathed Jean. "I'll get my husband to come and help me in the morning. I can do without a phone for one night." They both left the building and locked it up for the evening.

The next morning, Jean and her husband arrived early. She unlocked the building and went inside, turning on the lights as they headed over to the case.

"Trust you to drop it behind the biggest case," joked her husband. As Jean approached the case in question, she stopped in her tracks. Her jaw dropped and she looked at her husband. Sitting on the top was her phone. The building had been locked all night with the alarm on. No other members of the team had been in. Jean couldn't explain how her phone had got there but she had the feeling that Sir Henry was to thank. And so, she does just that every morning.

Outside in the grounds, many people have spotted a group of friars walking in a procession, one behind the other. One particular sighting stands out as unusual. A local man was walking the grounds one evening. He had passed a couple of people but he was now alone. Standing on a large square of grass, he was looking toward the castle ruins when something stunned him.

A group of hooded figures were walking along the path towards the castle. He took them in further. Their robes were brown in colour and their faces were hidden. He realised that they were not walking along the ground, but above it. Not floating, but walking, step by step over thin air. It appeared to him as though they were walking a path of their own. As if the ground they once knew, once walked on, was now much lower down. As the figures approached the castle, they began to descend into the solid ground. As if they were walking into a lake, getting deeper and deeper until they disappeared out of sight.

These hooded figures are believed to be Trinitarian Friars who settled in Knaresborough around 1252. The priory was built on what is now known as Abbey Road, a tranquil lane by the River Nidd. It was destroyed by the Scots in 1318 but parts of the ruins can still be seen today. Along this path is the cave of 'Saint' Robert of Knaresborough. Although he was never officially a saint, he lived in the cave as a hermit in the early thirteenth century. It is believed that, when he died, healing oils oozed from his gravesite.

Knaresborough, Fruit & Veg.

The shop on Silver Street, whose name aptly fits the products they sell, is not haunted. The flat above however is said to be home to a couple of ghosts. A family were living in the flat and all was well until, one morning, their youngest son came to breakfast. "I'm tired," he complained.

"Eat your breakfast," said his mum, Sarah.

"But the old ladies kept me up last night," he said, with a mouthful of cereal. His mum and dad looked at each and shrugged it off. "Just a dream lad. Now finish up," said his dad.

The same thing happened every now and again with the young boy complaining of two old ladies coming into his room at night. "They look kind," he said to his mum as she listened to him again one morning. "They don't do anything, they just come in and look kind," he yawned. Months passed and the family moved out for various reasons. They rented the flat to another family and forgot all about the old ladies. That was until the two families happened to bump into each other. "Hello," said Sarah. "How's the flat? Have you settled in now?"

Susannah replied, "Aye, it's nice enough but my little daughter isn't getting much sleep. She keeps complaining of two ladies coming in her room at night. She says they're not scary, in fact they look kind. Not sure what is going on but some of the door handles keep moving on their own as well. No one is ever behind the door; they just move on their own." Sarah had never told anyone about what her youngest son had seen in his bedroom, or about her own experience of moving door handles, but you can likely bet that the two old ladies are still haunting the flat today.

Waterside Old Manor House, Knaresborough

The oldest building in the town, which sits by the River Nidd, is unmistakable as it is painted like a chessboard. It is believed that when King John was in residence at the Castle, he would often leave his advisors beneath a great oak tree while he went off hunting in the Forest of Knaresborough. He built a hunting lodge around the oak tree in 1208, yet if you were to open a cupboard in the kitchen of the current house, you would find the gnarled trunk of the original tree inside. Some of its lower branches used to act as ceiling beams. These were removed at the end of the 20th Century.

It was during renovations in the early 1900s when a gruesome discovery was made that laid to rest two ghostly apparitions. A young lady had been spotted at the foot of the stairs. However, she was more often seen rather than heard; wailing and crying at the bottom of the old staircase. Her spirit was accompanied by the sighting of a ghostly cat which would often run around in the same area.

During the 19th Century, builders damaged a wooden panel at the foot of the stairs. Behind it, they uncovered a secret room with a macabre secret. Inside they discovered the skeletal remains of a young woman, parts of her dress and hair were still intact. What is

more disturbing was that she was entombed along
with a cat, whose skeleton lay beside the remains of
the young woman. No one knows who the young lady
was, yet locals have whispered rumours of a witch and
her familiar being interred there. The remains were
removed and given a proper burial, after which there
were no further sightings of the cat or the girl.

The house remains a private residence and in the
garden is a 400-year-old mulberry tree from around
1608, when James I was attempting to establish a
national silk industry. His plan failed however, as they
planted black mulberry which silkworms do not feed
on. James later gifted the house to his son and future
King, Charles I, who played a role in the Battle of
Marston Moor.

The Old Dispensary, Knaresborough

The Old Dispensary is a Grade II listed building and dates from 1853. It is situated adjacent to Knaresborough Castle in the centre of the town and has an unusual tale to tell. The story was featured twice in the local paper, The Knaresborough Post. In the article, Vonni Wilkins reports about the haunted house lived in by Mrs Mabel Watson. In the story, it is said that Mabel and her husband photographed a ghost in their house. The image shows a short man with a white coat and potentially a beard or large moustache. Two weeks later, the newspaper received a phone call from Mr Douglas Norton, who claimed the ghost was his grandfather, Obadiah Norton.

Obadiah was born in Cambridgeshire in 1832. He enlisted into the army where he served as a hospital sergeant in the 57th Foot Regiment, known as the Old Diehards. He saw much action in the Crimean War. He eventually moved to Knaresborough with his four children from his first marriage in New Zealand. He worked at the dispensary for thirty years until his death on June 22nd 1911, aged eighty. It is not known for sure that the ghost attached to the house is in fact Obadiah, but he certainly bears a resemblance.

In the 1960s, Mabel Watson and her husband lived in the house and she reported a lot of paranormal activity.

In one of the rooms, a door seemed to have a mind of its own and liked nothing more than to remain open. Every time Mable left the room, she would close the door behind her, only to notice it had later opened. She was vigilant in her mission to close the door and kept doing so, only to always find it open later on. Mabel began to get annoyed and, so it seemed, did the entity who was responsible for opening the door. One day after Mabel had closed it, the door flew open with such force and aggression that it caused the nearby piano to clang so loudly it sounded as though it was playing itself. Mabel decided to leave the door ajar from that day forward.

Mabel became increasingly aware of a presence in the house which she named Joey. She felt as though she was never alone and always being watched. One may have thought she was mad but her paranoid thoughts were only made real when a friend visited. With her, she brought her well-mannered dog who found comfort sleeping on the floor between the two ladies as they gossiped and caught up on much-missed news.

After some time, and without warning, the dog woke and sat upright. The ladies stopped talking and their eyes were up on the little beast. The dog's head looked toward the door, the door which liked to remain open, and its head seemed to follow something as it seemingly and invisibly crossed the room, walking towards an empty chair next to the fireplace. The usually placid dog raised its heckles and let out a deep, guttural growl, its eyes now resting plainly on the apparently empty chair. The two ladies exchanged looks. Embarrassed by her little companion's unusual behaviour, the owner gently stroked her dog, hoping to calm the animal. In response, the dog got up and ran the short distance to the chair where it let out a menacing growl. Unexpectedly, the heavy fire grate fell over towards the little dog who, losing all courage, whimpered back to its owner. This odd occurrence only solidified Mabel's belief that her house was haunted.

Later in the year, Mabel had new carpets laid. She was rather house-proud and would spend time ensuring the carpets were clean and tidy. As with most new carpets, once walked upon, they initially leave behind your footprints until wear and tear means this no longer happens. Mable walked from her kitchen to the drawing room. Turning to close the door, she noted the footprints she had left behind and was looking forward to the day when the carpet had worn in enough to stop this irritating effect. She sat and read for a while and, when she eventually opened the door, was taken aback when she spotted a second set of footprints on the carpet. She was alone in the house at the time so was utterly baffled by the footprints. These ghostly prints continued until the carpet had finally worn in.

After the passing of her husband, Mabel decided

Paul Forster

to take in lodgers to help pay the bills. The house was situated across from the police station and as such, there was a constant course of lodgers from the cadets who trained at the station. Much of the time passed without incident but, now and again, a lodger would come out with an unusual story. One such boarder was a young cadet, Neil Smith, who had been staying in the house for a few days. He was sitting in the drawing room reading the paper when another lodger entered the room. Neil looked up and greeted the man. "Hello," he said, but the man ignored him and sat down. Neil assumed he wanted to be alone but then why enter a room with someone in it? So, he pursued a conversation. "I'm Neil. Good to meet you." Nothing. "Have you been staying here long?" Still no reply, when the man got up and left the room.

Later that day, Neil spoke to Mabel. "Who was that other chap? The one who doesn't speak? He was rather rude to me earlier. Tried making conversation only he completely ignored me and left the room. Rather peculiar," said Neil, sipping his cup of tea.

"Other gentleman? I'm afraid you're mistaken. You are the only lodger in residence, my dear. It's just you and I. Out of interest, what did he look like?" asked Mabel. "He was a short elderly gentleman with a white beard. Oddly, he was also wearing a white coat. I thought he was a doctor of some kind." Mabel's blood ran cold. She did know who Neil was speaking of but he certainly wasn't a guest, not a paying one anyhow. The first time Mabel had seen this little man was at the top of her stairs. She was alone in the house; her lodger was at work when she heard a noise at the top of the landing. Arriving at the foot of the stairs, she looked up and on the landing was a short man with a white beard and coat fussing about. It looked as though he were moving unseen items around, almost as if organising things. She called out to him but there was no reply. He simply vanished.

Years later, Mabel's daughter was visiting from abroad. Mabel was thrilled that she was staying as she was bringing her new granddaughter, who Mabel was yet to meet. Mabel had all kinds of plans arranged. Tea with friends, a walk around the castle grounds and lots of cuddles with her granddaughter. However, as bad luck would have it, the little, one-year-old girl, was teething and colicky. It made for a tempestuous visit. Mabel had been through this herself with her own daughter so she knew they were in for some sleepless nights.

After the third night, most of Mable's well-thought-out plans lay in ruin. Her daughter had not slept for a few days prior to her visit and was looking exhausted. Mabel offered to take the baby so that she could rest and the offer was quickly accepted. Mabel eventually calmed the baby, placed her back in the cot next to her mother and took herself off to bed.

The next morning, Mabel woke feeling refreshed. There hadn't been a peep out of the baby all night. She went down to prepare breakfast for everyone. Later, her daughter arrived at the table, the baby in her arms. "You look very well rested my dear," Mabel said, kissing her daughter's head and stroking the cheek of her granddaughter.

"Thanks to you, Granny," replied her cheerful daughter.

"I really didn't do much, I was lucky she was so tired from crying most of the day that she fell almost straight to sleep. After I laid her down in her cot, I never heard another sound all night." Mabel poured a warm cup of tea into a waiting teacup; her daughter took a sip and shook her head. "Well, you did a little more than that, if it cost you anything then I am happy to repay you."

Mabel looked confused, "Cost me? I don't understand dear. What would have cost me?"

Her daughter looked up from her tea. "The doctor. He was very nice. He came in just at the right time. I think this little one was about to have another teething tantrum. He was very gentle, picked her up, administered something to her gums and said, 'There, you get some sleep.' I thanked him and must've fallen straight back to sleep. He may think me rather rude but I was exhausted. We should thank him with some tea."

Mabel stood stock still, teapot in hand, listening to her daughter. "Are you ok mum?" her daughter asked.

"What did this doctor look like?" asked Mabel, already knowing the answer.

"Well, it was dark but you couldn't mistake his white beard and coat. Short chap. Very friendly. Are you ok? You look like you've seen a ghost."

Years later, another cadet was staying at the house. A confident young fellow by the name of Joe McCabe. Joe was a large young man who was physically strong and healthy. He had been ribbed by the other cadets at the station because of his lodgings. They told him tales of a ghostly man who haunted the house. Joe didn't believe a word of it and was growing increasingly sick of the jibes. One night, a fellow cadet had joined him for some supper after a night at the pub. His mate, Gary, asked Joe if he had been visited in the night. Joe, rather loudly and brashly, said he thought that ghosts were a load of rubbish and if there was a spirit in the house, it would do well to stay clear of him, or else.

In the early hours of the morning, Mabel was woken by an ear-splitting scream followed by shouts for help. "Help me, someone. God help me!" Mabel threw on her night coat and rushed to Joe's bedroom door where she loudly knocked. "Joseph, are you ok? Are you decent? Shall I come in?"

"Please, yes. Come in, Mrs Watson," cried Joe.

Mabel opened the door and threw the light switch on, only to find that Joe was pushing the wall with his right hand. His other arm seemed to be stuck between the bed and the wall.

"I can't get my arm out," he cried, as he pushed the wall with his free hand using all of his strength. "My goodness, how did this happen?" asked Mabel with flushed cheeks. "Lord knows, but it won't budge."

"Shall I call the station for help?" she asked.

"No!" said Joe quickly, for fear his colleagues would have more ammunition to use against him. "I can move it." He tried again with all his might; Mabel even helped to pull the bed but it was of little use. Joe gave up trying. "It's as if something is holding it there," he said.

"Or someone," replied Mabel. And then, Joe, who had been trying to move the bed for some time, tried again and was suddenly able to move it and free his arm.

He sat up and rubbed his arm. "It's gone dead! Pins and needles!" he grimaced, as he rubbed the blood back through his arm. "Must've fell asleep with my arm hanging off the bed. I've done that before but I don't have a clue as to how the bed got pushed up against the wall." Happy that the drama was over and eager for her bed, Mabel walked back to the door and, as she was closing it, said, "Perhaps our doctor doesn't like being made fun of, Joseph. Sleep tight." And with that, she closed the door.

One story which came to light tells of a young girl at the house who was seriously ill. Her parents sat by her bedside, fraught with worry. A doctor entered the room and saw to her needs. Calmly and without a word, the doctor administered something to the child. Her parents looked on concerned. Thanking him, he left without a word.

The next morning, the girl had made a full and quick recovery. Both parents had assumed the other had rang for the doctor but, after talking, they realised neither had made a call. Confused, they phoned their local surgery to find out which doctor had come to their aid and thank them. The receptionist told them plainly that no doctor had visited their house, indeed, nobody had called them for help.

It seems that the mysterious dispenser, who bears a resemblance to Obadiah Norton, is a helpful and kind spirit. Perhaps even in death, the ghostly doctor is always on duty for those in need.

Scotton Banks Hospital, Knaresborough

Scotton Banks Hospital was built in 1937 as a long-stay Tuberculosis (TB) hospital however, when the need for the treatment for TB declined, it was turned into an NHS hospital in 1948. The building was sadly demolished in the 1990s. A housing development is now on its former site.

In the early 1940s, a young staff nurse named Evelyn was working alone on her night shift. They usually passed without incident, especially considering she was caring for those patients in the geriatric ward. She sat at her ward desk where she dealt with the night staff's reports and re-arranged any flowers left by visitors. She did this in the sluice room each evening. The sluice room was used to deposit any human waste from the wards and, although it sounded disgusting, it always smelled nice. It was probably one of the cleanest rooms in the hospital and Evelyn thought that the flowers probably helped mask any unpleasant aromas.

Stretching along one wall was a huge rack of bedpans. The rack itself sat at a 45-degree angle so that gravity held the metal pans in place. The room sparkled with cleanliness as Evelyn removed any lilies from the bouquets. It was hospital superstition that no lilies were allowed on the ward so they were gifted to a local church instead. Once she had finished, she turned off the light and locked the door. She walked through the silent building and back to the ward where she refilled the stationery on the main desk and replenished the thermometers in their jars of antiseptic.

Evelyn sat down with a sigh and began folding a few hand towels which needed replacing when an almighty crash of metal startled her. She stood up and looked towards the sluice room from where the racket was coming. She could hear the metal ped pans, clattering and spinning around its tiled floor. It made a terrible din and woke a couple of her patients. She gave them a gentle look and a kind smile as they rolled back over to sleep.

Worried that someone had perhaps broken in through the window and damaged the shelf, causing the bedpans to spill across the floor, she decided to call the night porter, Edward. He lumbered down the corridor towards Evelyn, who looked worried. Edward looked annoyed; having had his late-night reading rudely interrupted. "What seems to be the issue, Staff Nurse?" asked Edward curtly.

"There was an almighty crash in the sluice room, I think…"

"The sluice room?" interrupted Edward.

"Yes," said Evelyn. "The sluice room. I locked the door so no one could have gotten in there, so perhaps someone came in through the window?" she finished.

"Why would anyone want to break into the sluice room?" asked Edward.

"Well, I don't know. Let's go in and check," replied Evelyn.

"No," Edward said.

"No?" repeated Evelyn.

"I'm not going in there till morning," Edward stated and he turned and walked away.

"What? But…" Evelyn stood and watched Edward walk back down the corridor and out of sight.

Evelyn returned to her work but couldn't stop worrying about the potential break-in. She imagined the mess the bedpans would have made. Perhaps some of the tiles had been chipped or broken. Whatever the state it was in, she would be the one cleaning it up. The rest of the night passed without incident and morning soon came. Good to his word, Edward turned up at 7 am. "Right, let's get this mess cleaned up," Edward said as they walked towards the sluice room.

"You're going to help me?" asked Evelyn, not hiding her surprised tone.

"I'm a gentleman, Staff Nurse. Can't leave you to sort out all of those bedpans on your own. No doubt I'll have to fix the shelf too. Probably broke and spilt the lot of them across the floor." They reached the sluice room. Evelyn unlocked it and they opened the doors.

They both stood there in shock. They expected the

bedpans to be scattered across the floor but they were not. They were instead neatly stacked in rows across the centre of the room. They stood there, uneasy and unsure of what to make of it all. Edward simply walked away in silence leaving Evelyn to deal with the bedpans.

Old Royal Oak, Knaresborough

This 18th Century pub has an old-world feel and comes complete with a priest hole along with a number of ghosts. I visited the pub which has been run by husband-and-wife team Sharon and Rob Toon for nearly seven years. As soon as I stepped inside, the hairs on my arms stood up to attention. There was unusual energy in the building. I spoke to Rob first who eagerly took me to the cleaning cupboard. Not the type of place I would imagine we would find a ghost but I was wrong. Rob emptied the cupboard of some of its contents and spoke over his shoulder to me as he did so. "Under the floor is the old cellar. Cobbled stone floor with a capped-off well. This is also where the secret tunnel starts, goes right under the market square and off into the warren of tunnels beneath the street." He hefted a large can of cleaning fluid out of the way and revealed a trapdoor. "Now, the wife'll kill me if I open this because activity gets worse when we do. They don't like it when we open this hatch." Yet he did.

Rob stood up straight and shook, as if someone had walked over his grave. I soon followed and the hairs went up on the back of my neck. It felt as though a ball of energy had passed straight through us. Rob turned and looked at me. "I felt that too," I said.

"Aye, that'll be them coming out." Rob moved out

of my way and gestured to the gaping dark hole in the floor. I moved closer but was genuinely fearful. "Not nice, is it?" stated Rob from a safe distance.

"Not at all. So, what has happened down here then?" I got out my phone, stretched my hand inside the hole and began taking pictures. Rob answered, "Apparently a priest was using the tunnels one night and it collapsed on him, killing him. Whenever we open this, we usually see a black shadow figure passing through this area soon after. Could be the priest but who knows." I finished taking photographs and backed away to let Rob close the hatch, returning the cupboard to some normality.

Back at the bar, I looked through the photos on my phone. A few cobwebs were all I saw but, in one photo, there looked to be what could have been a spirit orb (though, on closer investigation, I think it could also have been a spider's web). Rob saw me inspecting the orb. "We've captured a load of orbs on camera down there. Not surprised you've caught one," he commented.

Just then, Sharon came out of the kitchen and joined Rob behind the bar. "You've not been in that old cellar, have you?" Rob shot me a knowing look.

"I told you. They don't like us going in there." Sharon seemed lovely but also not someone to mess with. A stern but friendly lady, clearly proud of their local pub. The couple lived upstairs with their dog as Sharon explained, "Our flat is above the pub and when we first moved in, they [the ghosts] tormented our dog. They would have him chasing his tail around and around in the middle of the night, I know that's something that dogs do but he'd never done that before and he's an old dog. Then they started taking his toys, hiding them from him, so he would run up and down the flat looking for them. They tormented him. They'd just turn up later on and he'd be confused. This was July 2016 but, months later, things got so bad I phoned my friend's father, Phillip, a Benedictine Monk who lives in Whitby. He told me some holy words to say and, that night, I called out to the spirits and gave them what for. I said these few words and they stopped. Only now they throw things down here in the pub. One dinner time there were a few customers in. One was an old bloke. I heard a glass smash and I assumed he'd dropped his glass. Only, when I went over to help him, he pointed behind the bar and said, '*It wasn't me love, it was over there.*' So, I goes behind the bar and on the floor is a smashed brandy glass in the middle of the floor."

Sharon went on to explain that a number of gin bottles had been thrown from the shelf on which they sat, seemingly aimed at bar staff, only narrowly missing their heads. Looking at the shelf myself, I noticed there was a brass bar, like a banister, which was there to stop bottles from falling off the shelf. So, anything which had come flying off this shelf must have lifted over this bar. On the cellar door is a plaque, now screwed to the wooden door. This is because the plaque would frequently be thrown at people passing through the door. One evening, a staff member, Andy, went into the cellar and the plaque hit his head. So now, everything in the pub is fixed to the wall. Anything which they cannot fix to the wall still gets thrown around.

One Friday evening after a busy day, Sharon, Rob and her staff had locked the pub up. They all helped lift the chairs from the floor, turn them over and placed them on top of the tables. The floor cleared; they then mopped the tiles. After this, they all sat in the lounge bar, enjoying a well-deserved drink and chatting. Suddenly there was a loud crash. Everyone stood up and looked over to the tap side of the bar. To their dismay, a number of chairs from different tables had been thrown against the pub door, breaking the glass, laying in a tangled heap.

The poltergeist activity taking place in the pub is a continuous onslaught of mischief. One night during the darts league, two young, local men were keeping scores at the bar. A pint of lager was lifted into the air by an unseen hand and the entire contents were poured all over one of the men. Every few months, the activity seems to be prevalent with glasses of drinks being knocked over or literally poured over patrons. Glasses are thrown across the pub, landing on the floor but never smashing.

At the rear of the pub are a number of well-decorated and homely bedrooms. These rooms were once the stable block and when Sharon and Rob moved into the pub, they heard rumours that a stablehand had hung himself in the barn centuries before. One night, when all was quiet and still, Sharon's ringing phone woke her up. Picking it up she was confused when a man started babbling and shouting about something horrible, he'd seen in his room. Once Sharon had calmed him down, he told her what had happened. He was staying in Room Four and had woken up in the middle of the night. There, hanging from the rafters, was a man with a rope around his neck. He could see him clearly as there was light coming into the room through the curtains. This has since happened around six or seven times during their ownership. Different men, women and couples telling the same story.

The paranormal activity is not just centred around Room Four. Next door, in Room Five, a number of guests have reported the same thing. After leaving to enjoy the delights of town, they returned to find they couldn't get back into their room. The key worked and turned the lock but, when they tried pushing at the door, it wouldn't budge. Rob would be called in to fix it. The first time this happened, he brought his tools to fix the lock, only the lock wasn't broken. He looked through the external window to the room and to his shock he saw that all the furniture in the room had been stacked and piled up against the door. After much pushing and heaving, Rob gained entry and put everything back in its place. This has happened on more than one occasion since.

Mr and Mrs Jones were the owners of the Old Royal Oak in the 1950s. Elfyn Jones and his wife Carys lived alone in the pub and they frequently experienced unexplainable activity. One night, they were both tucked up in bed on the verge of sleep when Elfyn nudged his Carys awake. "Listen," whispered Elfyn. Carys sat upright and stared into the darkness.

She could hear footsteps above them. They sounded heavy, like a man dragging his boots along the floorboards. They walked down what she imagined was the corridor leading to the attic door when they suddenly stopped. A latch unhooked and caused an audible clicking sound, then it fell silent. Months later, the couple's eldest son was visiting. He stayed in one of the rooms at the back of the pub. In the middle of the night, there was a banging on the couple's bedroom door. It was their son and he looked like he'd seen a ghost. He claimed that he had woken in the night and, in the moonlight, had seen a man hanging by a rope around his neck from the rafters above him. Terrified, he fled the room.

Paul Forster

There is little known about the hanged man in room four or who the poltergeist and other spirits and shadows are who haunt this old pub. But if you are looking for a drink and a spooky story when you visit Knaresborough, your best bet is the Old Royal Oak.

The End is Never Truly the End

Take a moment to consider that the stories you read were true. If this were the case then surely, they offer proof that there is life after death. Right? That is what many people hope. I believe that ghost stories are just that. Hope. They offer those left behind in grief, a little ray of hope that there is something beyond this mortal coil.

The spooky stories we tell are there to honour the dead. These tales help us remember those that have gone before us. They serve as a reminder that we will not be forgotten. They entertain and thrill but are they really real?

Ghost stories are very real for those who experience the event. Once the initial incident has taken place, they are nothing more than stories. If you've been on your own and experienced anything paranormal then telling someone else is a difficult step. You fear you won't be believed, perhaps laughed at or ridiculed. I know that's how I felt when I saw the ghost in cubicle 13.

Just like Sir Arthur Conan Doyle was a staunch believer in life beyond death, I too believe in something. I'm not sure exactly what this something is. It is the sensation that I'm not alone in an old house. It's the hairs standing up on the back of my neck and the little old lady I saw in the Turkish baths. The latter of the three is something that I don't think even science could have explained.

Science is something that we all use to explain the world we live in. When something is described as paranormal, it means that it falls outside of the normal parameters of scientific understanding. Some people believe that ghosts aren't real and that they are simply imagined. Or are they the result of some other-worldly factor? How do you explain the unexplainable? You can't. If every single one of these stories were all made up by the people who told them, then we are surrounded by some incredibly creative people.

Finally, it is thought that by simply talking about ghosts we can increase the likelihood that more paranormal activity is reported in a particular place. Once a story is in the public consciousness, it is more likely that other people will see, hear or feel things. So, by simply reading this book, you are more likely to experience something paranormal when you next visit one of the haunted locations featured. Next time you are in North Yorkshire, why not join me on my ghost walk and hear some of these stories first-hand?

I look forward to welcoming you to Haunted Harrogate.

Acknowledgements

Writing a book is hard but more rewarding than I could have imagined. It wasn't all down to me and without the support of others and stories from many people, I would never have written this book in the first place.

I have to start by thanking my amazing wife, Francesca. She has been so supportive of my freelance lifestyle and has put up with my endless ideas and money-making schemes. She was a great help with this book from reading early drafts to giving me advice on the cover to keeping our beloved son, Rory out of my hair so I could write. She was as important to this book getting finished as I was.

When I started this journey, I looked back at my childhood, growing up in a haunted house. It was through chats with my mum, Jean and my brother Michael that helped us all to remember the terrifying experiences we all had in that house. Thank you both for sharing those memories with me.

Thanks to Zachary Greaves for the introduction to my now publisher, if this hadn't happened there would be no book. I owe my deepest gratitude to the skills of both Cathy Harris and Lucy Cole for editing the first part of this book and making some great suggestions.

A special mention and a huge thank you goes to my

friend Gillon Hopson. Who, at my hour of need, was able to step in and edit the second half of this book for me. You are a great wordsmith and I look forward to new storytelling adventures in the future.

Thank you, Rick Armstrong, and all at Fisher King Publishing for taking a chance and believing that I could not only write a book but make the deadline on time.

Gareth Humphreys is owed a debt of gratitude. His talent for design saw him create the beautiful artwork for the cover of my book and it was a joy to work on it together.

Many people have contributed their stories to be contained within these pages. If I have missed your name, then please accept my apologies but know that I am eternally grateful. There would be no haunting stories without the following contributors: Mark Ellison of Knaresborough Knightmares Ghost Walks for your many spooky stories; Amanda Wilkinson and the staff at the incredibly haunted but very friendly Hales Bar; Karen Perkins; Kate Stead and her dad Conrad Stead who is now a believer; Rosemary Enright; Chris Myers (NYPI); Leslea Petty; Linda Lefloch; Paul Warner; Susan Murton; Jane Wharton; Katie Summersall and the staff at The Turkish Baths Harrogate; Joanne Mayben; Christopher Mark Emery; Sharon Toon and her husband from The Old Royal Oak; The Harrogate

Club; Helen West from The Crown Hotel; and finally Kevin Langford and your fantastic stories from the Odeon Cinema.

And finally… I would never have believed that one day, someone like you would be so willing to read something I had written. Please accept my sincere thanks. By the way, as you read this, was one of your legs crossed over the other one? If I was right, then please do let me know on social media @harrogateghostwalk or @forsterthemindreader.

I hope you enjoyed reading Haunted Harrogate.